CLARITY TAROT

Debra Zachau & Kait Matthews

REDFeather
MIND | BODY | SPIRIT

Copyright © 2022 by Debra Zachau and Kait Matthews
Library of Congress Control Number: 2021948667

All rights reserved. No part of this work may be reproduced or used in any form or by any means—graphic, electronic, or mechanical, including photocopying or information storage and retrieval systems—without written permission from the publisher.

The scanning, uploading, and distribution of this book or any part thereof via the Internet or any other means without the permission of the publisher is illegal and punishable by law. Please purchase only authorized editions and do not participate in or encourage the electronic piracy of copyrighted materials.

"Red Feather Mind Body Spirit" logo is a trademark of Schiffer Publishing, Ltd.
"Red Feather Mind Body Spirit Feather" logo is a registered trademark of Schiffer Publishing, Ltd.

Designed by Danielle D. Farmer
Cover design by Danielle D. Farmer
Type set in Abril Display / Obvia
Black circle frame and square shapes with gold stripes, gold spheres © CoolFinger_67. Courtesy of www.bigstockphoto.com.

ISBN: 978-0-7643-6373-3
Printed in China
5 4 3 2

Published by REDFeather Mind, Body, Spirit
An imprint of Schiffer Publishing, Ltd.
4880 Lower Valley Road
Atglen, PA 19310
Phone: (610) 593-1777; Fax: (610) 593-2002
Email: Info@redfeathermbs.com
Web: www.redfeathermbs.com

For our complete selection of fine books on this and related subjects, please visit our website at www.redfeathermbs.com. You may also write for a free catalog.

CONTENTS

- Introduction 7
- **What Makes This Deck Unique?** 8
  - Keywords on Love and Money 9
  - Easy Yes/No Answers 10
  - Timing Is Everything 11
  - Rich Cultural Images 13
  - The Design 14

Part One: How to Use This Deck   15

Part Two: What's in a Number?   19

- **The Suits with Their Elements and Superpowers** 38
  - Wands 39
  - Swords 40
  - Cups 40
  - Pentacles 41
  - The Suit of Wands 44
  - The Suit of Swords 51
  - The Suit of Cups 60
  - The Suit of Pentacles 70
- **The Court Cards** 80
  - Kings 81
  - Queens 82

- Knights 82
- Pages 83

Getting to Know the Families' Personality Traits of Each Suit 84

House Number One, the Wand Family 86
- King of Wands 89
- Queen of Wands 90
- Knight of Wands 92
- Page of Wands 93

House Number Two, the Sword Family 95
- King of Swords 97
- Queen of Swords 98
- Knight of Swords 99
- Page of Swords 101

House Number Three, the Cup Family 103
- King of Cups 105
- Queen of Cups 106
- Knight of Cups 107
- Page of Cups 108

House Number Four, the Pentacle Family ... 109
- King of Pentacles 111
- Queen of Pentacles 112
- Knight of Pentacles 113
- Page of Pentacles 114

Part Three: The Major Arcana 116

0. The Fool 118
1. The Magician 119
2. The High Priestess 120
3. The Empress 121
4. The Emperor 123
5. The Hierophant 124
6. The Lovers 125
7. The Chariot 127
8. Strength 128
9. The Hermit 129
10. The Wheel of Fortune 130
11. Justice 131
12. The Hanged Man 133
13. Death 134
14. Temperance 135
15. The Devil 137
16. The Tower 138
17. The Star 141
18. The Moon 142
19. The Sun 143
20. Judgment 144
21. The World 145

Part Four: How to Give Awesome Readings 147

Following Your Intuition in Readings 150

Spreads and Throws 154
- The Celtic Cross 155
- Five-Card Yes/No 157
- Timing Spread 160

Cheat Sheet 161

Serving the World 170
- Hotline Advisor 170
- Event Psychic 172
- Stage Entertainer 173
- Animal Communication 174

Final Words 175

INTRODUCTION

Welcome to the *Clarity Tarot*! Kait and I have had such a wonderful time creating this deck and have enjoyed bringing the secrets of Tarot into the light so everyone will feel comfortable hearing the messages clearly from spirit. We have unique challenges in the 21st century, and now, with this deck, you have a way to navigate the complexities for yourself as well as for friends and family. If you have a desire to serve as a professional reader, this deck provides Spirit with the right tools to communicate in a clear and concise way.

WHAT MAKES THIS

There are five components that are unique to the *Clarity Tarot* deck that will ensure you understand what the cards and Spirit are trying to tell you (then through you to your client). You will also garner deeper awareness and greater knowledge from this deck of 78 beautifully illustrated cards. You not only know what spirit is trying to tell you but *how to say it* in a way that is completely unbiased, centered, and supportive of someone who may be needing direction. It's one thing to know the message; it's another altogether how you say it that supports a person and what they are going through.

It takes practice to give a reading that isn't filtered through your own experiences, challenges, and residual fear left from your own personal setbacks. This deck, along with the teachings available online, will remind you how to stay above the lower frequencies and within the higher octaves so you can do good work and be of good service.

Divining the future and taking a peek at the trajectory of either your own life or the life of

DECK UNIQUE?

another is exciting, and you may be interested to know you can also learn mediumship by using this deck. If your fascination is a desire to communicate with passed loved ones, this deck is a good tool for that as well.

Kait and I created this deck with five specific ways you can read so your energy will never get tired or jaded. There are many doorways into your intuition, and I have created five still points that will ensure you always do good work when reading.

Keywords on Love and Money

With the keywords conveniently placed and easy to read on each card, you needn't have to question if your answers are coming from your imagination or your intuition, since you can be sure your answers are always coming from your intuition. The keywords will keep you on track. Allow your vibration to remain high while your eyes pick up the words and phrases smoothly, allowing spirit to draw the insight in your mind that will be most helpful for your client. The most-asked questions are about love, while the second most popular are money and career. You will find keywords for both at the bottom of each card.

Easy Yes/No Answers

I always receive the proverbial yes/no questions, which with all honesty can be answered with a simple coin toss. No one is satisfied with just a yes or no answer, so this deck answers not only yes or no but *why* the answer is yes and *why* the answer is no! You will notice at the top of every card there is either a "Y" or "N" corresponding to either "yes" or "no." You can lay down an odd number of cards (I commonly use five for this reading) and just count how many "yes" and how many "no" cards you laid down. To understand what influenced the answer, simply read the keywords correlating with the topic of interest. As with any modality there are exceptions, so I suggest you look at each card before giving the answer, since the message from spirit may be for you and how to talk with your client, and not so much for the client. I will explain the nuances of this component throughout this book.

We all know the future is not set in stone and is always moving and malleable. The reason people enjoy psychic readings is to see what their most probable future is, but some don't understand the most important thing. If a person isn't completely happy with the answer, then all they need to do is make a change at the level of action to influence a shift. To be clear, if the answer they're searching for is disappointing in any way, then the cards actually tell you what a person may need to do at the level of action to possibly change their future to an outcome more to their liking.

"Yes" and "no" answers can be tricky, and you need to frame the question well. More about this in *How to Give Awesome Readings*, found in this book as well as classes online.

Timing Is Everything

As mentioned above, psychic timing is tricky since the future is constantly in motion. There are a lot of moving parts because we share space with many personalities, all of whom are making their own free choices, including some that may influence us and our path. Someone's actions will create consequences for us, most often our spouse and close family.

Our various and complex personalities, mixed with situations with varying degrees of emotion, give us impulses to make choices, sometimes unhealthy ones. The quality of our choices relies on our moods and biases, and it helps so much to be able to reference something like the Tarot that is always centered and practical.

When asked for a timeline, simply shuffle the deck and start laying down cards one on top of the other until you reach a major card. That major card will have a number on it: that number will be from 0 to 21. You will then use your intuition to decide if the time increments are days, weeks, or months. As an example, if your timing card is Strength, you will see the number 8 on the right side near the border. All you do is tap into your intuition and have spirit tell you whether the answer is eight days, eight weeks, or eight months.

Rich Cultural Images

The *Clarity Tarot* has yet another component that makes it easy for the advisor to pick up little clues that spirit wants you to know. It's in the rich cultural images. Tarot is a very old form of divination, and traditional decks hold traditional Old World biases, especially within the court cards. The court cards represent the people who are influencing your life, and in the days of old, everyone's skin was white and the color of one's hair determined if they could be trusted or not.

Here you will find a rich and diverse format more congruent to the world we live in today. Our deck celebrates all cultures. If perhaps the cards predict that your client may be meeting someone new and she or he asks what the person may look like, this unique aspect along with your intuition may be able to describe small traits to keep an eye out for. I'm not one to take all the fun and surprises out of meeting someone new, because some people filter out everyone but those with all the traits you put on their list. But with these wonderful images there are always a few things I feel comfortable describing.

The Design

The next unique part that will make you a success as a Tarot reader is the design of each card. Kait Matthews has brought together an exquisite combination of colors, symbols, and images in a collage that inspires and delights not only you the advisor but your clients as well. When working quickly on the hotlines or at events, I am able to use this deck effectively since it is designed for upright readings. The keywords have enough information of caution and direction for a reader to do good work.

HOW TO USE THIS DECK

PART ONE

You can start reading right away! You will be able to practice your intuition and start reading just from learning the personality each number has, as well as the elemental meanings of each suit. If perhaps you have a reading with a lot of cards from one suit, then spirit is telling you something very important.

Learn the two parts of the deck: the Major and Minor Arcana (*arcana* means "mysteries"). The Minor Arcana are the numbered cards (ace through 10) as well as the court cards (also known as the family), consisting of Kings, Queens, Knights, and Pages. The Minor Arcana represent the everyday events (ace through 10) and people in a person's life (the court cards).

The second part of the deck is the Major Arcana or mysteries. These are 22 special cards that come up throughout a reading to encourage all involved to use a higher perspective around the questions. Think of the major cards as advice from spirit regarding your client's situation.

Build upon that by creating a relationship with each of the cards. A description for each of the 78 cards is included in the guidebook. As you read, it would be in your best interest to look at each card to start forming a personal connection. It's vital when developing confidence to understand the language of spirit as you move through a reading.

Next we will explore the different ways we lay down cards known as throws or spreads. There are many ways to cast a throw, and you can make up your own as well. The premise is that every card has a place with a specific meaning that shows how it influences the topic or question. A common one is the past, present, and future three-card spread. The first card is the direct past (two to four weeks prior to the reading). The present card will tell the influences for the situation as it stands now, as well as what your impulses may be. The third card shows the most likely future in two to four weeks. Keep in mind while sharing this information, a person can decide a different plan of action if that forecast isn't what they want.

If a card is thrown down reversed, that's another way spirit wants to communicate. It doesn't necessarily mean the opposite of the upright meaning. This deck is designed to read the cards upright, but I like to leave the reversed cards as they land when I throw. If most of the cards are reversed, I ask myself if spirit is telling me the question is framed correctly, or if it is asking me to talk with the client first to make sure we have the same intention. That being said, if there are just a few reversed cards, then I read it as a possible block or restriction the client might be placing in front of themselves, and the reading will identify and clear that up. Clients will, quite often, ask what another person is thinking about them or about a situation. This information helps them better understand how a good friend or partner is feeling, and once armed with this information can bring understanding and harmony to an otherwise challenging situation.

So don't be too quick to turn the reversed cards upright when doing a reading. It just may be your angels, teachers, and guides asking you to think differently before beginning, in order to provide good-quality information and an awesome reading.

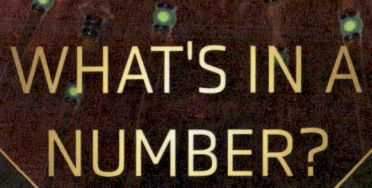

WHAT'S IN A NUMBER?

PART TWO

Knowing the power of each number is the first step in learning the language of Tarot. Learning how to recognize the energy of a number will serve you well. If you have time to learn only this section and the section on what the four suits mean, you are close to stimulating your intuition's true north, which will allow you to connect to your Higher Self. That way you are calling in an abundance of confidence in your new language with spirit. After being introduced to how an event can equate to the energy of a number, you can start identifying values and priorities in complex life situations.

Ace

If you draw an ace (or 1), it means the beginning of something wonderful. It can also be spirit encouraging you to retreat into some alone time to celebrate your sovereign way toward a peace-filled heart. Aces can also indicate new projects, jobs, and love interests, and a myriad of activities that are fresh and new. It could mean new beginnings of concentrated energies with strong impulses to act. This number also indicates clarity of purpose and fresh actions to complete unfinished tasks or create new goals altogether. Aces can represent the idealists of the world, since the impulse to start something usually stays in the thinking mode (with the exception of the Ace of Wands) and sometimes stays suspended in the mind, where no harm can come to the situation or project. A good example of this is the person who knows she or he has a great book in them and will get that book on paper someday. If the book remains in the mind, that person will never have to endure the pain of a poor review or rejection from a publisher. The supporting cards in the reading will give the reader a clue as to what will or won't become a reality. The Ace of Swords is a symbol of thought with new ideas bubbling out. Unless the client puts pen to paper jotting down all those ideas, then the project will remain in ace energy. The Ace of Pentacles is the new path being created in regard to material wealth and acquisition. The Ace of Cups is head over heels in love with a person, project, or direction, to the point where—if not recognized and monitored—it can push a person into pure, off-planet fantasy about the direction of their life. This is when many mistakes can be made in regard to love. Last but not least, and the one ace that actually brings an idea into the world fast, is the Ace of Wands. There is very little time between a idea and putting that thought into action.

2s

The 2s will point to partnerships and unions. They can also represent your relationship to spirit. Because the 2 follows the ace, it can mean a positive continuation of what was started. The 2 means you are forming an alliance to something or someone. It can indicate you are balancing your mind, body, and spirit. It says you are understanding another or can see a project that can be shared for a better outcome. It indicates positive collaboration. People with a lot of 2s in a reading can be experiencing trouble with boundaries since they can't figure out where their energy stops and another begins. A person insisting on harmony at all costs may be exhibiting the shadow side of 2s.

This type of person tends to anticipate another person's needs and to address those needs before their partner even knows what she or he wants. Most often this will leave this lovely, giving soul feeling quite unappreciated.

The 2 of Swords shows a stalemate in a situation where no one has all the answers or solutions. Both are weighing out possibilities. The 2 of Cups is the symbol of existential love partnerships even though it represents collaboration on all levels. Most readings are about love, so I address it here and elsewhere in this writing. The 2 of Cups shows mutual attraction and the balanced awareness that both will move forward and explore a relationship. The 2 of Pentacles shows a person is balancing the monetary commitments better than they think, and the 2 of Wands shows smooth progression in an active project, expressing assurance that whatever decisions you or your client face will put everyone on the right track and to keep going.

3s

The 3s are all about how you express your emotions. They signify the progression of a project in proper course. Self-expression is the key when you have a 3. You must search outside yourself to find people who will mirror back your best self, but the trick is not to be defined by other people's opinions. The number 3 is the master communicator. It shows how you react to your art, song, book, or presentation of ideas. You are now reaching outside yourself and stretching. It's a beautiful progression from the single ace to the collaboration of the 2 and the expression in the 3. We bring possibility into reality and become cheerleaders for everyone. This number is the first big risk anyone takes with their heart wide open. In the Tarot the 3 of Pentacles is the apprentice doing good work and fully embracing a new career path. The 3 of Wands has an open heart with supporting progress of action with self and others. The 3 of Cups means happiness while celebrating your personal style of expression with friends and the world. Last but certainly not least, the 3 of Swords reveals your first deep disappointment finding yourself on a razor's edge between despair and faith. Whichever side you fall on, remember that it is only a 3, and you can and will rise above what broke your heart.

This master communicator will find a place for this hardship, storing it safely in your list of experiences, where it will not return to sabotage you in the future.

4s

The 4s bring all the above possibilities and anchor them here on earth, in reality. The 4s are easy to remember, because you can't roll a four-sided block. The 4s are always stable and stubborn; think of the four corners of a foundation being a stable and solid structure. Self-discipline and organization come with this number. Wherever you are in life, a 4 asks you to find firm footing in regard to emotions (to be even and centered) and choices (to be well thought out before acting). If you happen to be in a stable relationship or job/career, this number is requiring you to pay attention to what is around you to keep the success going. Keep extremes off to the sidelines. If you are not in a place, situation, or relationship of your liking, it's time to make reliable plans for a more secure future, keeping in mind that all changes should be made slowly. If there are several 4s in your reading, spirit is saying that the place you are at this moment will demand a different way of thinking. Move away from unsettled situations by using logic versus emotion. Make decisions with your head not your heart. Seek out guidance from a wise one if you find yourself in the energy of the stubborn 4. The 4 of Pentacles is rethinking wealth and possessions, and the 4 of Swords is knowing when to withdraw and rest from the world. The 4 of Cups is cautioning that your indifference in a relationship may be causing conflict. The 4 of Wands shows a firm foundation regarding the security you have built and surrounded yourself with.

5s

Whatever isn't working out through the first four numbers will be brought to light with the 5s. The number 5 represents shifts and changes, and most people are not fond of change, even though that is the only thing in life we can count on. When 5 is around, certain areas in your life will have *just enough* disruption to cause *just enough* discomfort and give you *just enough* impulse to make a decision to change. Catch this early and you won't be sorry, since what isn't working will become crystal clear. Change the tide or get caught in the constant cycle of disruption and chaos. This is the ultimate freedom number, which has a tremendous curiosity with it. People are information driven and start to look forward to new experiences in every area of life, as long as they let go of what isn't working for them. Thoughts and quick wit are yours, and you become distracted by all the shiny objects in the world. You can't seem to settle on something to commit to. Life is too exciting to just stay put and in one job, one relationship, or even one career. The 5s do well in the spotlight and find traditional careers, relationships, and any job where someone else says when to show up terribly inconvenient. The demands of relationships, whether romantic or professional, are added pressure and give the feeling of living under the gun, making it very hard for 5s to play by traditional rules. Take the 5 of Wands: this card represents gossip and possible mean-spiritedness of others and will produce that indescribable icky feeling when you enter a room or meeting. The 5 of Pentacles catches you skipping over gratitude and into a feeling of loss. The 5 of Swords gives an impulse to cut important corners on a project or relationship, skipping important details. And the 5 of Cups creates a feeling of regret and remorse. More than one 5 in a reading will signal change in multiple areas in a person's life, and the reader would be wise to move through each suit slowly since the client may be overwhelmed with their lives at that moment.

6s

The 6s are about balance and harmony, caring for others, and being community minded. Once you start seeing 6s come into your reading, you can be sure conflicts will calm. When 6s are present, it is spirit suggesting you take a breath, stop, and slow everything down. You will be able to evaluate misunderstandings, even having enough peace within your heart to see your own part in the problem. The number 6 is a gracious number, a loving number, a peace-filled number that will move self-centeredness to the background and the desire to serve others forward. If perhaps the 6s inside your reading are reversed or ill dignified, take note that the option to move into this blessing is still very much available to you, and you are advised to consider the effort it may take to move away from petty conflict and into peace. The 6 of Cups is family of origin and sharing good memories from the past, while the 6 of Wands tells you the world has noticed your good works. The 6 of Swords shows you calm waters are ahead, and the 6 of Pentacles grants a philanthropic or generous energy to your heart.

7s

The 7s indicate tremendous intuition and spiritual growth. A person will automatically want to turn inward with their thoughts. Often I remind clients if I see their reading heavy with 7s that not every thought they have will be their own, since they very well may be picking up other people's bad moods and worries. Have you ever been working at your desk, having an okay day, when all of a sudden you feel crummy for no reason? Yep, that's 7 energy in action. Know what is yours, and energetically send the other stuff back to where it came from. I suggest prayer to angels, teachers, and guides to help with this. If it's left unacknowledged, you may find yourself acting out other people's anxieties, causing unnecessary challenges and misunderstandings in your own life. The 7s bring the desire for solitude and soul searching. The opportunity this brings is substantial, since the barriers shielding you from the answers to why things have happened in your life are thinner and more understandable. Look deeper into metaphysics as intuition and mediumship skills begin to sharpen and become easier to understand. Paying attention to the specific suit of 7s in a reading will give information that will serve you or your client as it signals which path out of a challenging situation shows the least amount of turmoil. The 7 of Cups asks you to meditate or simply allow your mind to be open to all possibilities, understanding that not all you receive at this time is meant to be manifested now; nonetheless, the huge amount of information you receive will serve you in future endeavors. The 7 of Wands encourages you to stand your position even if you aren't sure why right now, so trust it. The 7 of Swords warns of a tricky situation that will need grounded action and straight thinking. Not everything will make sense at this time, so don't make decisions that can't be easily revised. And the most balanced of all the 7s is the 7 of Pentacles. Your intuition regarding commerce now bears fruit. You are certainly not at the end of the road regarding wealth building, and work still needs to be done, but you are on the right path.

8s

The 8s indicate material wealth, leadership, and public recognition. I have discovered when 8s show up in clients' readings, their minds are not as focused toward love partnerships unless it is in regard to owning a business together. It doesn't mean they aren't in love and completely devoted to their love partners; it means they are focused on discipline, honor, and dedication to a material project or team. People with 8 in their readings won't be romantically overt, and some partners may think that the love is drifting away from the relationship. This isn't true at all; it just means that their person has a mind filled with acquisitions, investments, and what kind of car to buy. They are anchored in the material, which isn't a bad thing; heck, that's why we have all decided to incarnate on this dense planet—to have fun with the material world! All the food, the money, and the ability to build concrete structures—even artistic expression—are anchored in the 8 energy as it brings something undefined (an idea or inspiration) into the defined. An emotion is captured in a tangible way onto a canvas, or a poem or a play. An 8 represents organization or the ability to organize and manage as you develop big ideas or concepts. When 8s appear, you have a huge amount of potential available, but to bring success you must bring forward your sincere devotion and dedication. This goes for projects and partnerships of all kinds. Since the suit of Wands is always fast-moving energy, the 8 of Wands reflects the momentum, with a profound sense of urgency, and can even indicate air travel. The 8 of Cups brings the knowledge of what is solid and reliable and what is not. You walk away from something you have devoted time and energy to but leave with honor and a sense of achievement. You have learned all you can from this 8, and now you are leaving it. The 8 of Pentacles offers opportunity to study your fascination and then bring it into fruition with little effort. And finally the 8 of Swords is where your mind and beliefs limit you into believing you are at no choice and can produce no forward movement.

9s

The 9s mean you start to let go of what isn't working in order to hold your peace. It's time to back up from your focus on what *should be* or, worse yet, *must be*, and to let go because at this time it's dead weight dragging you down. Get rid of things so you can breathe. The blessing will be a new outlook on life as a whole, and you will be granted the ability to see a much-bigger and much-clearer picture. Not heeding the notice to relax your grip on things will drag you down fast and for long periods of time. The 9, much like its counterpart the 6, stands for humanitarianism, altruism, and understanding. With understanding comes tolerance and patience. By now, with this mature number, you have learned not to sacrifice yourself in the processes of serving the world. The 9 is the last of the single digits and represents the end of a cycle as the wise prophet who has accumulated all the knowledge of the first eight numbers. The 9 of Wands shows that the service to another is uneven, and the surrounding cards will tell you whether this time of hardship will be short or long lived, as well as telling you whether this extra effort, for the sake of another, is truly necessary at this time. It sometimes signals a partner serving their person during a personal challenge and for the sake of the relationship commits to an unbalanced portion of responsibilities for a while. The 9 of Cups shows that your wishes come true and celebrations are in order. The 9 of Pentacles shows an independent sovereign being in wealth and security, comfortable with their accrued possessions. The 9 of

Swords (thoughts) has a person up at night, all in their head ruminating on regrets of the past or fear of the future. It's a valuable card when doing a love reading signaling someone who cares deeply and is disturbed by the situation enough to lose sleep over it.

10s

The 10s indicate the maturity and end of one project and the beginning of a new one. When the 10s show up, you can be sure that you have said and done all you can say and do with a particular situation or person. It's time to light up a new path and start looking toward a new horizon with a bounce in good fortune. When a 10 or multiple 10s settle in your reading, life is telling you that a decision must be made and that a step forward in any direction (doesn't have to be the right direction) must be taken now. We experience stagnation in our lives, and if a 10 shows up while in that state, we may have to really push ourselves to do something—anything—and there may be some discomfort in the decision-making, but the promise of a new, more positive life will make the efforts easier. The 10 of Pentacles represents material family lineage or inheritance. It is material wealth, possessions, and wisdom a group or family has accumulated through shared efforts. The intentions are to have this knowledge and tangibles be offered to the generations to come. The 10 of Wands shows you are finding the anticipation of a new burden larger than you feel you can handle. Understand you have gained all the knowledge of the first nine numbers, and you have more than enough tenacity to take on the new path before you. The 10 of Swords is a hard ending to a cycle, one that uncovers a betrayal and may leave you exhausted. This is one of the most challenging cards since it pulls the curtain back to reveal how others have truly felt or what others have done without your knowledge. The opposite is the 10 of Cups, showing domestic bliss where you find yourself comfortable and safe within your own life and trust the people around you.

If only our lives went in a straight line like this! You wake up every morning with an ace in your pocket, and by nightfall you tuck yourself into the understanding and acknowledgments of the 10. Well, life is a bit more complicated than this, and lessons are learned by the bumps in the road and not so much the smooth surfaces. Understanding what numbered energy pattern you or your client have created and may be stuck in can help shine a light on the lesson to be learned, setting a person up for softer days.

The SUITS with Their ELEMENTS and SUPERPOWERS

Each suit has a dominant color to help differentiate it, as follows:

WANDS: red/orange; the element is fire and the focus is action. Literally physical motion.

SWORDS: shades of blue; the element is air and the focus are thoughts.

CUPS: bright gold; the element is water and the focus is emotion.

PENTACLES: shades of green; the element is earth and the focus is the material world.

Wands

This is the fastest-moving suit in the deck, with the symbol of fire and the focus of action. This can mean that whenever a Wand card is close to any other card of any other suit, there seems to be a quickening in regard to when events or decisions are made. This suit wakes you up and gives you the extra strength you need to get a beloved project done, file the papers, start the schooling, or finish mowing the lawn. Wands are the fire under us that helps us achieve our highest and best. Wands represent enterprise, career creativity, and inspiration.

If there was a horse race with four horses, one horse representing each suit, then the wand horse would come in first by many lengths. When you do a reading heavy with wand energy, you can be sure there is little time between the thought of doing something and actually doing it. The blessing this suit brings is motivation, while the darker side can sometimes manifest in a quick temper, with words and actions that may cause regret after the situation calms.

Swords

The suit of Swords owns the element of air, with the superpower of dynamic thought pointing to a very bright and sharp mind. Situations are still quite fast as the race horse carrying the Sword label will be the second to cross the finish line. The blessing is clear thinking, while the other side is worry and anxiety or too much negative thinking. The suit of Swords holds the most challenges, as you will notice once you start doing readings. Thought will trigger so many emotions, and once we are swimming in that, the challenges are compounded into blocks and restrictions. Too little or too much of this suit can cause problems, so it's important to have a friend or confidante to help you talk out your thoughts and ideas with impartiality and centeredness. Not feeling so alone in a stressful situation where your thoughts run away with you can sure help.

Cups

The suit of Cups presents the element of water, and its dominant color is gold, an easy color to love because Cup's superpower is emotion. This is the third-fastest horse to cross the finish line, since emotions tend to slow a person up a lot of the time. The suit of Cups represents all emotions: the good, the bad, and the indifferent. Emotions of all kinds are represented here, with the blessing being love and the shadow side, indifference, and folly (making decisions both large and small only on the basis of emotions), which never serves anyone well. You may experience so many longings you can't tell which thoughts are based in reality. Deep emotions can give way to fantasy and uneven expectations of your partner both in love and business. It's best to keep your head over your heart when being pulled into deep emotions.

Pentacles

Last but not least, the horse that comes in dead last is the suit of Pentacles, since it carries the heavy element of earth. The dominant color of each Pentacle card is green. This card represents all the ticktock, mundane, tangible items in your life, as well as situations that move slowly, such as the tedious building of careers and relationships. Pentacles represent all the objects in your life, such as the sofa you're sitting on, the car you drive, and the money you have in the bank. Whenever you have Pentacles in a reading, the timeline is slower because the suit revolves around our day-to-day lives. The blessing is abundance and business success, with the not-so-fun side of greed and hoarding. Basically the blessing is gratefulness, while the dark side is the complete opposite of not feeling grateful, and leaning into jealousy and envy.

Now that you know a bit about the numbers as well as the personalities of each suit, let me introduce you to each card so you can create a clear emotional correspondence with each. I know you will fall in love with some right away and will remember their meanings—some will even become your favorites. Others may not give you a feeling of deep connection until they appear in a dynamic and profoundly moving reading where real understanding grows and becomes a part of who you are as a reader. Once you start learning the meanings,

these 78 cards will become quite familiar and you will begin to trust their message every time you work with them.

THE SUIT OF WANDS

Ace of Wands
N

Since our Wand suit has the element of fire and fast-moving energy, when you see the Ace of Wands you know there is a call to physical action. This is the beginning of the exercise program (commonly appearing close to the beginning of the year as resolutions abound). This is active inspiration in the form of creativity.

A reading about love has the keywords of *new joy/love/creativity*, and if the topic is money, new creative projects.

2 of Wands
Y

2s always indicate partnerships and collaborations. Most often the 2 of Wands shows a person progressing well in their chosen path. An all-around happy card.

Keywords for love are **building a rewarding relationship** and, for money, **beneficial guidance from others.**

3 of Wands
N

Most often the image is a person looking out to the next horizon, sometimes looking over land or calm water, which represents a progression of actions. It has been my experience that when the 3 of Wands appears in a love reading, it most often means the person of interest is in another country, travels for a living, or you are communicating through the internet.

Keywords for love are **commitment/engagement** and **celebration** and, for money, **efforts bear fruit/others help.**

4 of Wands

Y

This is one happy card! Remembering the personality of the number 4, you have strong foundations with efforts leaning in traditional ways regarding both work and family. This indicates a strong foundation is building and is an especially welcome card. Having the 4 of Wands appear signals that both parties are serious about the relationship. I have seen marriage proposals when this 4 is in a reading.

Keywords for love are *happy* and *comfortable home/contentment* and, for money, *success/harmony/stability*.

5 of Wands

N

Remember 5s are change and will shine a light on what *isn't* working in your life. The image on this card shows people in a defensive stance with their wands pointed at each other, but notice none are touching. This is the classic low burn of petty gossip and the annoying actions of short-tempered snaps toward friends and loved ones. It's true that 5 is a relatively low number, but make no mistake: too much of this on a daily basis will corrode joy right out of your life.

Keywords for love include ***bickering/let go of ego.*** For money, *tensions at work* and don't engage with ***gossip.***

6 of Wands
Y

This shows the worst is over and people are noticing you with respect and appreciation. Sometimes the meaning of a card will shift when certain other (mostly major) cards are present. For the most part this card shows a balance of self-confidence and humbleness. If a poorly aspected card shows up next to it, the meaning can shift to self-centeredness and being too proud. As a stand-alone card it is a welcome sight for people who have worked hard at a task or project.

Keywords for love are **time of happiness** and **encouragement** and, for money, **well-deserved success** and you **are being noticed.**

7 of Wands
N

As you can see, the woman on this card is determined to have things her way. She has all she needs to make sure that whoever wants to challenge her physically or mentally will not get past her high mound and firm stance.

Keywords for love suggest a *big ego / try seeing the other's side.* For money, this 7 encourages you to *hold your ground* and *diligent work.*

8 of Wands
Y

This card represents going in a straight line with speed and light-hearted freedom. The 8 of Wands points to spontaneous action without thought. This card shows the energy of the topic moving so fast it can actually indicate air travel. If this card is teamed up with another card that points to family (6 of Cups, 4 of Wands, 10 of Pentacles), my intuition will tell me that my client may be flying to a family reunion. I mention these little tidbits when I have found some combination to be true so many times that I always tell a client about it. If it doesn't ring true for the moment, I suggest they put the information in their pocket and look at it again later. Nine times out of ten, that family reunion invitation shows up in the mail.

Keywords for love are an opportunity for a *sudden interest / fast and passionate* and most likely unsustainable, and, for money, *split-second decisions and rapid gains.*

9 of Wands

N

The woman who is pictured in this card has all her wands lined up and in perfect order. Whenever I see this card I happily inform the client that the worst of their hardship is over, success is near, and not to give up.

Keywords for love are **resolving challenges with partner.** As for money, the 9 of Wands recognizes your hard work and says **the worst is over and stability ahead.**

10 of Wands
Y

This card highlights that the burdens in your life are weighing on you. If there are pages (court card), this 10 points to the responsibility for a dependent person, who can be a child or an adult who is unable to help themselves. I sometimes see this 10 when the responsibilities of the partnership or marriage are uneven due to one person having an illness or employment challenges. This 10 tells you that spirit sees your hard work and is sending help.

Keywords for love tell you may be of **support to a partner in hard time and uneven care.** Keywords for money are may have taken on too much and **feelings of** burnout.

THE SUIT OF SWORDS

Ace of Swords
N

Indicates a new way of thinking and focuses on a new idea of some kind or that a new idea is on its way. Mental clarity is yours, and you will triumph over any adversity. A positive card, especially if it is well aspected with Wands, since it would show not only a great idea but motivation to action as well (certainly a combination to look for).

Keywords for love include ***rising above adversity/healing*** and, for money, ***inspiration, possible new job,*** and ***clarity.***

2 of Swords

Y

This beautiful card shows a soul taking a break from all outside influences (blindfold) and weighing out options (two swords crossed). Swords are all about thinking over things, then thinking them over again. This 2 means that decisions may take awhile and that there is a slowing and possibly a complete stopping of forward momentum. The message is to not push a person with the 2 of Swords in their reading, since you will end up getting nowhere with the conversation.

Keywords regarding love are **pause for balanced thinking on situation** and, for money, **have faith in your own ideas and wisdom.**

3 of Swords

N

This impressive image shows broken hearts due to quarreling. Sharp words spoken or kind ones unspoken cause a disappointment or letdown that deeply changes opinions and may even shift the focus on how you relate to each other in the future. Even though this 3 is shocking and can set a situation back or stop forward motion in its tracks, I remind clients that this card has only the energy of a 3. Every card has power and its own place and purpose, but a low number like a 3, even with a challenging situation, means the relationship has a good chance of surviving.

Keywords for love are *quarreling but union worth saving* and, for money, *loss of trust/ unhappy job* situation. Remember that all cards are transient, and no one is stuck in a challenging season unless she/he chooses to hang on to resentments.

4 of Swords

Y

You've been through a lot, and the 4 of Swords says it's time for a rest. I love this card when it comes up because I get to tell my clients that they can relax, that the worst is over. You can see with this beautiful illustration that all her weapons are at the ready, but she can sleep for a while and the angels are saying, "We got you."

Keywords for love include holding an unsurprising message of ***much-needed time for self*** and, regarding money, ***rest after hard work / burnout.***

5 of Swords

N

If you haven't caught on by now, the suit of Swords has the most-challenging cards holding the most conflict in the deck, with the 5 of Swords representing a match of wits and intellect. Sword cards represent headstrong personalities with axes (or swords) to grind. You want to guard against loss and deceit, whether it is someone else causing this disruption or an uneasiness inside yourself that may lead you to cut out important details on projects that really should have your full attention. A person can lose compassion for a loved one when this 5 appears. Be mindful of who is around you and of your own thoughts and impulses for possible gaps in personal integrity.

Keywords for this card regarding love are ***arguing is not the answer / careful*** and, for money, ***avoid arguments and enemies.***

6 of Swords
Y

Ah, right when I get you used to the idea that the suit of swords is challenging, life provides a safe haven in this 6. You are now moving into calmer waters, and the angels are saying, "Take the day off from worry; we'll take it from here." The most comforting message is "Be still; all will be well." I really love the way Kait illustrated this card, since there is a guardian assisting us and the family can simply be at rest in each other's arms. This reminds us that we don't have to go it alone, and when we discover peace, our frequency can hold up and positively affect others if we surrender to it.

Keywords regarding love for our 6 of Swords are ***moving into calmer waters*** and ***cooperation.*** The keywords for money are *work situation improving.*

7 of Swords

N

And now we move back into a bit of trouble. This 7 informs us that there is a situation that needs to be handled with care. When this card is coupled with a few other cards—namely, the suit of Pentacles—where money and possessions are involved, it could be a sign of dishonesty or even theft. Check your pockets to make sure your belongings, investments, and holdings are safe.

When this card appears in a love reading, the message is to *seek compromise* and *use diplomacy*. **When it shows up in a money reading, it *warns against moving forward / that risk is high* on a deal or project. Take a break and recheck things to ensure smooth roads ahead.**

8 of Swords

Y

This card shows a person all wrapped up in their personal assessments of lack and limitations. Even though it looks like someone else put those ropes around her and placed her in a jail of daggers, it's all her own limited thinking that has her feeling trapped. Quite often this card will appear when people find themselves in a marriage that is emotionally bankrupt, but because of the situation shows being dependent on finances or children or perhaps both; the person is prevented from leaving the challenging predicament. Many times, to find relief, all we have to do is back up far enough from the situation to see past the four corners of it. There are always options! Look to the horizon and see them, then make a plan.

This 8 has these keywords for love: you may be *feeling you have no choice / trapped*; for money, *fear of change* and you may feel your *hands are tied.*

9 of Swords

N

This card shows lots of worry and can actually indicate sleepless nights, so make sure you ask how your client has been sleeping. Spirit uses this card to remind people that they are watching and care about their health both physically and mentally. The suit of Swords has everything to do with our thinking, and this card tells us that you or whoever you are reading for is overthinking a topic or project and even blowing it out of proportion. Worry will throw a thread of doubt or fear your way with a little hook at the end of it, and if it's set just right, it can keep you up for days wondering, "What if?" When this 9 shows up, you should acknowledge the mental struggle your client is under, and then remind her/him that no one has ever crossed a bridge before they've come to it. The right words will come at the right time to the right people, so you don't have to rehearse it. Go to bed and get some sleep.

Keywords for love warn you may be *feeling rejected, lonely,* and *undervalued*. For money, it's indicating *regret and anxiety / feeling drained*.

10 of Swords
Y

Feel like you've been thrown under the bus or betrayed? People who pull the 10 of Swords may feel under the gun for no reason. Or they have a suspicion that someone has it out for them and may be setting them up to fail. If I'm asked how a coworker feels about my client and the 10 of Swords shows up, I most often say that the person in question is not their friend. There's a competitiveness about the person that they aren't being honest about. Of course one card does not make an entire reading, and there should be a few other cards to support a statement like that, but this particular card can really stand apart, and to dismiss it would be a mistake.

Keywords for love are **strain from caring for others** and, for money, **feel under pressure** and *suspicious.*

THE SUIT OF CUPS

Ace of Cups

N

The wonderful world of emotions! But Cups are not only the up and down emotions; they are filled with the full-bodied flow of creativity and intuition. This is the suit of expressing how we feel about ourselves and others, and the Ace of Cups is here to start the ball rolling into something brand new and passionate. It's the unique experience of love at first sight, the feeling of finally getting to work in the field you've been studying, or the special feeling you have seeing your child born. This is a joyous card, and one of great promise. If your client is a single person and the question is about love, you can be sure they will be meeting someone new, not someone blasting back from the past. If the question is about love and your client is already in a relationship, it will indicate a deepening of that love, a new depth of commitment.

Our beautiful ace has the keywords for love that show ***a new path to love/passion/purpose and, for money,*** *a new creative job* or project with a feeling of ***fulfillment.***

2 of Cups
Y

The 2 of Cups is the card that may indicate an old friend coming back from the past, since it shows a familiarity. This is a card of mutual respect and common ground and harbors a feeling of equals or peers. This collaboration gives a person an awareness of high hopes and inspiration. If perhaps I'm reading for a client and the question is "Will I meet someone soon and start a great relationship?," this card will tell me that the great relationship looks quite hopeful but most likely it will be with a person they already know. Not necessarily an ex-partner, although that could be the case, but someone they have already been introduced to at least once.

Keywords for love are harmony, balance, and *mutual respect* and, for money, *financial partnerships where you inspire.*

3 of Cups
N

This is a fun one since it suggests social interactions with celebrations. This is the "Let's go for a beer after work" card. It's the "carefree group event where no one is excluded" card. If I'm reading for someone who is looking for a partner and the 3 of Cups comes up, I know they will meet either at a group event or be introduced by friends. No matter where in the spread this card lands, it's meant to give an impulse to the recipient to get a group together to have some laughs or coordinate a night out with friends. These little lighthearted gatherings are built into our lives for a reason. Let your hair down, have fun, and remember we are better together; isolating is not in your best interest right now.

Keywords for this fun one are *socializing with friends / kindred spirits* and, for money, *profits through group efforts.*

4 of Cups
Y

So as we move away from the party with the 3, we go into ourselves with the 4. It's not a card that indicates alarming difficulty such as depression (it's only a 4, a lower number), but a feeling more like a blah indifference about things. I have found this to be true when reading about love and relationships. This blah attitude means boyfriends, girlfriends, spouses, et al. are not paying attention to details. It doesn't necessarily mean they don't love you; it means they're just plain lazy. This card is a bit different if the topic is business, jobs, and money. Then it can indicate a fixation on one thing to the exclusion of everything else. I have discovered that for love questions there is an indifference for *all* things, and for money there is an indifference on all things *except* one.

The keywords explain it better: for love, they are **withdrawing affections** and *indifference*, and for money, **attached to money and security.**

5 of Cups
N

So, in our image we have a few of our cups tipped over and wasted, yet there are still two cups close by that are full. As the image clearly explains, there is a disappointment of something, and the only way we would know that is to know what's in those cups. So how do we find out what someone may be disappointed in? How the question is framed and the quality of the cards around the 5 of Cups will point to what is causing the troubling feeling. If it's a love reading, someone is feeling bad about what was said or done. If it's work related, it's about not feeling fulfilled. Since we're getting higher in the numbers, the situations and answers become a bit more complex, and people start backing up further from their disappointing event and wonder what they've done to cause the sadness.

The keywords for love are **regret/remorse/some resentment** for what they have said and done, and, for money, you are **feeling unfulfilled/don't throw good money after bad.**

6 of Cups

Y

This card has everything to do with family and long-ago friends. This is a regenerative card with refreshing memories of Mom's apple pie and family BBQs. This card reminds us of our happy times of the past that raise our frequencies for a happier outlook for the future. It reminds us that we always have a home, even if that home is just a warm memory that helps us move forward. One of the curious things I have found from readings is if this particular card is dealt reversed, there is a feeling of separation from family or even a complete severing of ties. Remember that not every reversed card has the opposite meaning; however, in my experience, the reversed 6 of Cups representing a separation or a break of family has been true.

This beautiful card has the keywords for love that suggest *reunions* and *indicates* old friends and family and that the *conditions in your life will improve*. For money, you will enjoy a *renewed enthusiasm* for your project or work and *improved finances*.

7 of Cups
N

This card has many beautiful cups floating in front of a lighthearted, giggling soul who has her choice of any of them. It indeed means that you may be offered or will recognize many options in front of you. Be mindful around this playful card, since it indicates that not all of those options or ideas are based in reality. The person you are reading for needs to do a bit more research or look for a new perspective before making a choice. If this was a private client, they would have an opportunity to express their hopes and dreams in regard to all those options, and I would have the time to read on each of those options to help her/him make a sound decision. However, if I was reading for clients on a hotline, where time is limited, I would encourage them to research everything before moving ahead. Even waiting a week before making up your mind can bring about a higher chance of success and security. The 7 of Cups makes it clear that whoever this card is for doesn't have all the facts or is practicing mental and emotional escapism.

The keyword for love is very clear: you are ***indulging your fantasies;*** for money, you need to *examine choices carefully.*

8 of Cups
Y

The 8 of Cups is an empowering card for the person who receives it in a reading. It indicates that the person you are reading for has decided to leave a situation or project that doesn't bring out the best in them anymore. It says that they have put a lot of time and effort into it and looked at it as a lifetime commitment or investment, but the decision has been made to leave. The perfect example is when you wake up one day and realize you can't stand your job or career choice. You went to school for it and climbed the ladder to where you are, and you can't do it any longer. The good part is that when this 8 shows up, the decision is made and a sigh of relief that the challenge is over is enjoyed.

Keywords for love are ***walking away from love / a project***. You are tired of investing time into situations that just don't give back. And for money, ***cut your losses*** and ***conserve.***

9 of Cups

Both the 9 and 10 of Cups are beautifully welcome cards in any placement in any reading. Remember that when the numbers get higher, the experience is deeper and more profound. So the 9 of Cups shows a woman in an apron carrying a basket of flowers, possibly a shop owner or innkeeper, with nine upright cups, each holding great promise. This is the wish card, the card of joyful optimism while sharing optimism with others through celebrations of all kinds. A generous nature of sincere goodwill.

Keywords for love with this beauty are **rewarding love / contentment** and, for money, **new job/position or promotion.**

10 of Cups
Y

As mentioned with the 9, the 10 is another positive card with a little different flavor. The 9 is happiness and optimism for you and being offered to others through you, while the 10 of Cups is a statement of happiness and optimism for your family, extended family, and close friends. This shows the person you are reading for has a profound sense of gratitude and well-being with life in general. If that person is having a hard time, this may be spirit inviting you to shine the light on what they're grateful for by naming off a few blessings they have in their life. It's like spirit is asking you to start the reading there, at gratitude. It's a time to acknowledge that sense of belonging we enjoy when remembering there are friends and family who care and want the best for us.

Keywords for love are *a loving, joyful relationship* and, for money, *rewards, respect, and success.*

THE SUIT OF PENTACLES

Ace of Pentacles

N

The Ace of Pentacles (material) is the beginning of something tangible. Unlike with Cups (emotion) or Swords (thought) or Wands (action), you can actually hold a Pentacle. It's the money in your pocket, the car you drive, the person you live with, and the certificate on your wall—all the stuff you can touch and hold. A good way to remember the difference in energies is this: a guitar you can hold in your hands, since it's tangible (Pentacle), but the *thought* that went into writing the music (Swords) and the level of *emotion* that was expended while singing the song (Cups) while *strumming* the strings (Wands, action) during the performance are nontangible, and you can't hold those. The tangible and nontangible together make for a beautiful experience (unless of course it happens to be a nine-year-old and his first tuba).

Keywords for love are **meet through work / practical person** and, for money, **practical venture / profits.**

2 of Pentacles
Y

The 2 of Pentacles is the proverbial balancing act of budgets, savings, and possessions. Because it's a 2, with its duality, we have to remember there might be someone else involved, someone helping you out on a financial level or someone supporting your well-being on a practical level. If the reading is about money and finances, you are basically juggling your resources and you aren't feeling all that rich, yet you're not all that poor either. If perhaps it is a love reading, someone looking for love, the 2 of Pentacles points to meeting someone at work or someone who knows the client's industry well. If perhaps the client is already in an established relationship, this card could be pointing to the couple collaborating on a project or business, and it's prospering.

Keywords for love are ***shared resources / working with love partner.*** Keywords for money are ***juggling projects in collaboration.***

3 of Pentacles
N

This 3 shows you are very good at what you do or in your chosen career path. Whenever I see the 3 of Pentacles, no matter what the topic of the reading, I take a moment to say to clients that they are very good at what they do, and people notice and aspire to do things more like them. It's a work ethic and diligence that shows up when you are a novice destined for journeymen in short order.

Keywords when reading about love are ***stay positive*** and ***work through your differences*** and, regarding money, ***good at your work*** and ***people notice.***

4 of Pentacles
Y

The 4 of Pentacles is sometimes interpreted as someone being greedy or holding back their money in a negative way. Through my years of reading for others, I have discovered that this card represents a person who has been in lack and is now just above the waterline regarding financial comfort. You'll notice that the image on this card is a beautiful women who is holding a pentacle and has one pentacle behind her, and beneath her she stands on two. This card clearly illustrates a person who knows where all of her resources are. It has nothing to do with being greedy or stingy, but a practical card that shows smart management of finances.

Keywords for love are *stable/secure*, and you enjoy *love and status*. Keywords for money suggest you play it safe / secure job.

5 of Pentacles
N

The image on this card shows a couple who are sad and empty-handed. Remember this is a tangible suit, so they feel they are at lack, yet all they would have to do is turn around and see the light and warmth coming from the building behind them. This card means you have been overspending. If this card was in a future position, it may be indicating that a strong impulse to overspend might be coming. Remember that people get psychic readings to figure out what their most probable future is. Forewarned is forearmed, but I need to remind you that this is only a 5, so nothing catastrophic, yet you should pay attention to it because over time, overspending small amounts can lead to bigger problems.

Keywords for this 5 regarding love are ***giving lots*** but not feeling like you're ***getting back***. And for money, it cautions to ***trim down your lifestyle for a while.***

6 of Pentacles
Y

This card is best described as Scrooge *after* he was visited by the three ghosts. It's not only a time of financial security and abundance; it's also feeling so happy that you become a philanthropist, a generous person. Keep in mind the spiritual perspective of this card. Some of the least fortunate have the spirit of the 6 of Pentacles. You don't have to be rich to feel rich and have the impulse to be of benefit to others. This is balance and harmony and can indicate mediation when talking about legal matters.

Keywords for love are **sharing resources** where **both benefit** and, regarding money, **financial backing** available and **teamwork.**

7 of Pentacles
N

The 7 of Pentacles gives a feeling of accomplishment for your efforts. You will notice a hardworking person in overalls, with the shovel tending to what seems to be a money tree. When you see this card, spirit is telling you to acknowledge the hard work the client has invested in the topic. When I see this card in a love reading, spirit is asking me to acknowledge how much time and effort my client has put into the relationship. If in a reading about money, because this is Pentacles (material), it indicates the person you are reading for has invested successfully, pointing to retirement and other long-term investments that compound. This is self-made money or money set aside to ensure security. This card can also show an impulse to start letting go of things to free up resources.

Keywords for love are **small steps to improvement** and, regarding money, you are finally **starting to see gains** for your efforts, so **don't give up.**

8 of Pentacles
Y

This card reflects a maturity regarding a person's ability to create wealth, mainly because of a great work ethic. Reflecting on how the number makes a difference; take the 3 of Pentacles, for instance. It shows the novice studying the craft while the 8 of Pentacles is the journeymen, the teacher.

Keywords for love are **dedicated to each other / mature love** and, for money, you may be **getting a raise** but you definitely have **respect and gains.**

9 of Pentacles
N

This beautiful card shows a deep feeling of satisfaction, well-being, comfort, and success. You have what you need and much, if not everything, of what you want. This is a time to enjoy your hard work and a time of plenty. It's a job well done and goals achieved. You have a reason to be proud of yourself and can stand on your own, showing independence and sovereignty. This is the card I see most often with clients who are comfortable with their lives with or without a partner. There is a lot of emotional freedom in that, and I hope everyone gets to enjoy what that feels like sometime in their lives. Nothing else feels quite like being comfortable in the world by yourself.

Keywords for love are exactly that: *content with or without a partner;* for money, *acquire property* or a time of *profit* and possible *retirement*.

10 of Pentacles

Y

This wonderful card represents family money and inheritance of property. This is money not specifically earned by you, as represented in the 7 of Pentacles. With the 7 of Pentacles you are growing your own, doing your own thing, getting your own paycheck, and setting money aside for your own retirement. The 10 of Pentacles represents money shared from another's efforts—a financial windfall that wasn't yours in the making. When doing a reading where this card is positioned in the future, you do not want to say, "Oh, I see an inheritance coming your way," because customarily the only way someone can inherit something is if someone close to them dies, and of course we can never predict that. So the word *inheritance*, even though it sums up and speaks of family money and material wealth handed down, can be problematic. However, it means family of origin (mother, father, aunt, uncle, brothers, and sisters) and can be read in that context. It represents the family home along with fond memories. Early in my career, I would take notice that if this 10 was reversed, I would ask my client what the family relationship was like at that moment, and every client would say it was strained or nonexistent. So after thousands of readings, if this 10 is reversed, I'm comfortable assuming the emotional health regarding the client's family ties is not positive at that time. I would simply read with that in mind instead of bringing the topic up, if it isn't a part of the specific question.

Keywords for love regarding this 10 are *secure family life / legacy* and, for *money, wealth/family* and *inheritance*.

THE COURT CARDS

So now you know the individual numbered cards that represent a person's everyday life. The second part of the Minor Arcana (mysteries) are the court cards. These are commonly known as *the family* because they represent the people in our lives, the different personalities that influence and help us or hinder us on our path. They represent fathers, mothers, siblings, friends, enemies, bosses, aunts, and uncles. The royal court cards are the Kings, Queens, Knights, and Pages.

Each court card has personality traits, reflected by their suits, that bring to the reading specifics about who is influencing the client's situation by either being supportive or disruptive. Knowing the different personalities of the court cards is invaluable because you can accurately assess whether someone in your client's life can be trusted or is not deserving of that trust. You can look behind that person's eyes to find their intentions regarding each situation.

At times, an advisor will interpret the personality of a specific court card as a persona adopted by the client, so instead of the card representing a real human being, they will interpret the card as an attitude adopted by the client.

The Knights and Pages can be interpreted as messages instead of people, and practice will help you discern which is which. Extra information regarding these nuances as well as how you develop your intuition around them will be explained in the ongoing classes online.

Kings

Generally men over 40. If reading for an older man, I identify this person as a peer, a father or father figure, a boss, or someone in upper management. When reading for someone under 40, Kings can represent much-older siblings, since some families have big gaps in ages. The specific suit of each king will express his personality and disposition.

Queens

Generally a woman over 40. If reading for an older woman, I will read this card as a peer, a mother, or a mother figure, and as with the Kings, sometimes I read them as management in the workplace. A dominant woman need not assume she is domineering but simply considered older and wiser. Personalities of these beautiful women are determined by their suit.

Knights

Men or women above 18 and below the age of 40. In most decks, including this deck, Knights appear with horses to make sure the reader remembers to think of these people as movers, either bringing in information or taking it away. They represent the average adult male and female who are in their most active stages of building wealth, love, and wisdom. As mentioned earlier, the personality of each Knight is determined by their suit.

Pages

Pages are dependent children who can be either gender. What's interesting is that with all the years I've been reading, I have discovered that dependent adults, such as an aging parent or grandparent or the severely disabled adult that the client is responsible for, will show up as Pages in a reading. Pages are messengers of their suit. When Pages show up, I first think of them as children rather than messages. I can't tell you how many times a Page will show up in a reading about divorce, and it will start the conversation about a child who is having trouble with the changes in the family.

GETTING to Know the FAMILIES' PERSONALITY TRAITS of EACH SUIT

Understanding the different personalities of each family first will help you remember the individual court cards. Indulge your imagination for a moment and draw in your mind's eye to a short neighborhood block with only four houses, each having a yard. Each house belongs to one of our court card families. Imagine each family member having the traits of that suit. The fun part is, if you can keep up with this presentation and spend a bit of time with it, you will get to know the personalities of each suit as well as each person. Some of the descriptions will sound just like someone you know, and that's the magic of this exercise! That's when you really start a relationship with the cards, and the correspondence begins with spirit in such a confident way. If perhaps the description of each of our court family members doesn't remind you of someone you know, then think of a character on TV or someone who exhibits those traits in a movie. You now have a real relationship with the cards. So here we go.

HOUSE NUMBER ONE, THE WAND FAMILY

In our imaginary neighborhood we have the Wand family home, which will be quite busy (action suit) and always up later than the rest of the block. Enjoyable projects and seemingly never-ending chores keep them going from one thing to another, but never having the patience to complete a task. There are always clothes both in the washer (to be dried) and the dryer (to be folded and put away). Each family member goes into the dryer to shop for something to wear, taking it out and pulling it on for the day, leaving the rest. Not because they are lazy, but because they don't have the time to fold everything. The mother of the family will say yes to everything: need someone to pick kids up from school or something from the pharmacy? She's your gal, and she loves it! Although she may forget one of the kids or part of your order, she will certainly have her heart in the right place. She loves to be of service. The whole family enjoys exercising, either at a gym or doing outside activities. They will be more solitary in their actions and enjoy being a bit different in their step, both intellectually and on a creative level. Outside activities are favored as a family or just as a run by themselves.

Speaking of family gatherings, when you have a large number of Wand energy in the room, you can guarantee spirited conversations and even actions. Indulging in adult beverages and other commonly used coping items will exacerbate and intensify the drama. This family's dramatic ways can manifest both in positive and not so positive ways.

Every family has its tipping point into anger and upset, but the Wand family seems to have their set point in the range of little to no tolerance. An exciting time at the neighborhood block party to be sure.

The Wand family will most likely own their own business, and the details of all the different aspects of their lives will blend into one. Conversations about business and work are freely discussed at the dinner table, and projects meant for work are done at home instead. Multitaskers all of them, and with that, their attention to detail sometimes comes up short.

Their yard will be filled with toys that were dropped when another interest or idea popped into the kids' minds. Gardening projects, while often artistic and beautiful, will still have trowels, shovels, and gloves tossed around the scene, and some of the newly purchased flowers will remain in their plastic cups until wilted and spent. There's just not enough time in the day for this family. The Wand family didn't invent the wheel, but they did make it smoother and faster with their unique creative spirit and need for speed.

King of Wands

The King of Wands most likely enjoys work as an entrepreneur, independent contractor, or leader of a large company. He is happy to work alone and, on occasion, can be found leading a community event, but for the most part he enjoys his solitude. If he works for big business, he will be the rainmaker or the most successful in his department due to the volume of work he can accomplish. This King is not the fastest of learners (as his mind struggles to focus), but he will be the most productive. As we all know, the highest-quality works of art come out of the highest quantity of art making. As a father he can be torn between supporting his kids' activities and some project of his own where he can lose himself in the process of creating. He changes gears quickly, which comes in handy when you have little ones. He is mostly upbeat and happy, always finding it a bit hard to decide what to commit to, be it a project, a career, or a relationship, because the feeling of freedom is so important to him. Committing to something or someone means feeling overwhelmed by the expectations of other people's wishes and desires. That's when this charismatic free-form personality can show the harsher side of this character. At times of emotional struggle this King has a quick temper and can make destructive comments because he can't find the time to think things through.

Keywords for love are **affectionate and passionate man** and, for money, simply **good fortune through action.**

Queen of Wands
N

This beautiful queen may work more than one job and fills the rest of her time with family and creative work. If there isn't enough variety at her job or she isn't given the freedom to express herself, she will grow cynical and vindictive. When at work she dreams about all the things she could be getting done if she didn't have to be at her desk. She will add a gym session before or after her day job and use every bit of daylight doing activities she loves, leaving the chores she doesn't enjoy undone or done haphazardly. Dinners for the family will be creative, full of hot-spice flavor, and prepared fast. She is the person who, if perhaps having an extra 10 minutes, will choose to fit in a 20-minute task. Yes, this dynamic creative woman will be late to events for the most part and often exasperated and frazzled upon arrival. She is an artist, independent contractor, or entrepreneur and a mother who gets on the floor to play with her kids. She rarely gets blue or melancholy because there are so many projects she is passionate about. She's the person friends call if they need someone creative to solve a problem fast, since this Queen is never without a solution.

Keywords for love are saying this woman is **romantic / loyal / always busy,** and, for money, she reminds you of your **creativity / do what you love.**

Knight of Wands

N

This Knight represents a man or woman who is on the move and very creative as well as inspirational. This card can symbolize a message that the client will be moving or will be physically active. Whenever I see this card in a reading, I ask if the client has thought or is thinking about moving residences or offices at work. People who this Knight exemplifies tend to grow tired and bored of the same surroundings, in a shorter amount of time than most. If doing a reading for someone regarding career or job, it can signal a physical change of some sort. It can manifest as a new office, building, or company. Metaphorically, if the client seems settled in their work/career, this card may point to the client being offered a new creative project. Speaking about this Knight's personality, you can be sure everything is in high speed and revving up like the rest of this suit. Again, this card represents both genders and has a sharp wit and quick actions in everything she or he does, including making a decision and then jumping quickly into executing it. The age of this group is over 18 and under 40, a very productive time in a person's life in regard to settling or not settling down and starting a family. Of all the suits, this is the person with the trait of finding it difficult to settle and stay in a long-term progressive relationship. The Wand family members, more than any other suit, will likely have the most-blended families, since change comes easily for them, coupled with the anxiety of commitment, so this gives way to an eclectic family tribe.

Keywords for this mover and shaker regarding love are *enjoyable uncommitted affair,* and, for money, the card suggests you *take the risk / action is favored.*

Page of Wands

N

Pages represent messages coming quickly, as well as a young person under 18 or dependent in some way. For instance, during a reading if this page or a page from any other suit comes up, I ask, "Is there a child or someone dependent on you—a parent, neighbor, or possibly a friend in need?" Like I mentioned earlier, most times there will be a young one, but other times the client will be focusing on someone they feel responsible for. That being said, this dependent is the most active of the suits, always into something and not able to prioritize in concise ways due to youth, dementia, or disability, physically or emotionally. They can be the life of the party and enjoy lending a hand. They bore easily and are very hard to keep entertained. They may have difficulty in school due to short attention spans or the inability to resist interrupting, not to mention those wiggly feet.

Keywords regarding love describe a *playful, honest relationship* and, for money, *new skill or investment.*

HOUSE NUMBER TWO, THE SWORD FAMILY

Next door lives the family that *did* invent the wheel. They are the intellectuals of the block. Their yard will be a bit plain, and even though they have plans to have it professionally landscaped, they overthink whom to hire and how they want their yard to look. The design can be overanalyzed, or a stubborn family member may insist on researching further and maybe hiring more than one professional for the job. Lots of options come to mind that hamper the process of most of their projects, and this is one of the most baffling aspects of the Sword family. They are smart and educated and can overthink everything, so nothing ever gets done. When they do agree to move forward on an idea, they will leave it to the professionals to do, since they are much-better supervisors/managers than laborers.

The Sword family has great communication skills and enjoys spirited debate; for the most part they will respect the other's perspective, as well as talking things out if a problem happens to develop. But make no mistake: their truth will always sit inside the facts of any topic. They enjoy all matters regarding the processes of the mind and where science meets spirituality.

Inside the home we have lots of books and electronics, everything needed for research, because all are so curiosity driven. They are so wrapped up in their individual projects that the room will be dark long before someone thinks to turn on a light. Diet will be practical and nourishing, but there won't be a formal sit-down family dinner time. They do become closer when this family discovers one task, topic, or activity enjoyed by everyone. Once everyone knows their various tasks and place in the hierarchy, this becomes a well-oiled machine where great memories are created.

This family will be the one that is the hardest to get along with in regard to their neighbors. While the Wand family does everything with great speed, the Swords need very good reasons why something is done; it just has to make sense first. To dramatize the difference between the first two families, during the preparation for that block party the Swords will strategically plan out where the tables, chairs, and grill will go in direct relation to time of day, angle of the sun, and well-researched wind direction. The Wand family just sets everything up and starts dancing to the music.

King of Swords
N

This is a well-structured man who has a plan for everything. He studies his next step before taking it, and you will find he is or was very comfortable with his military service and most likely, upon retiring, went into another career that is highly structured, such as law enforcement or back to school to study law. Following the rules is an important character trait he looks for in others. He is bold and bright and his direction giving insight can be profound; however, if his wise information is not heeded, he can become harsh and bitter and will retreat.

This suit has everything to do with the intellect, and this King, as with the rest of the family, possesses a fairness and objectivity to any situation and would do well as a mediator or judge. What comes along with this is the ability to communicate well both in speech and the written word. He can appear stern when he is analyzing, and the engineering field would serve him well.

Queen of Swords

N

This beautiful Queen corresponds to the King of Swords, the difference being she leans more toward the creative side. Whereas the King may feel comfortable with numbers, this Queen is a wordsmith and has the ability to write for profit.

She is an independent soul who enjoys a sovereign life, being comfortable with or without a partner both in business and personal lives. She has learned from the hard times, and one would be wise to listen when she shares her knowledge.

I like to equate all the court card personalities to people I know or people who play certain characters on TV and in movies. It's a great way to become familiar to the nuances of each personality, and whenever that particular card shows up, you have a mountain of information to share with your client. I call the Queen of Swords the Judge Judy of the deck. She is smart, quick, and for the most part even-minded on her cases; however, she can cut you to ribbons in a matter of seconds. She can turn from pleasant to sarcastic to downright cruel in short order.

Keywords for love are smart independent ***woman*** and, for money, ***educated powerhouse.***

Knight of Swords
N

This family member is a fast and bright adult man or woman who will think things through before leaping into something. Whereas there is little time between thought and action with his counterpart (the Knight of Wands), the Knight of Swords will make sure all information and facts are in before moving forward. But you can be very sure when this Knight decides on a direction that he will get there in short order.

With hierarchy highly respected, the military life will complement this type of person. As with any fast-moving energy, when a situation gets moving too quickly, many upsets can occur. From the many readings I have done, when I see this card reversed I know that the communications between all concerned in any situation, be it business or pleasure, will be near chaos, with emotional immaturity pushing itself around, making things very challenging. I have found that just pointing this out, so the client can clearly see how far into the madness she or he has gone, will be enough information for them to regain their emotional footing.

Keywords for love are **shifts in relationship** and, for money, **finance or job shift.**

Page of Swords
N

This is a thoughtful message coming in filled with information, or a dependent child or person who is very bright. This one notices details and will never miss a word or dismissive look. This dependent's personality can put you through your paces when a conversation shifts from casual to intellectual to debate style, and you will be lucky to hold your own. I named the Queen of this suit the Judge Judy of the deck; the Page of Swords is the Sheldon Cooper of the family, the lovable character staring in the *The Big Bang Theory* TV series. He is incredibly smart but will hold everyone up if things aren't just right. If the group wants to go to the movies, Sheldon slows the momentum because everything needs to be just right. He is so busy mapping out the best time schedule to travel, eat, and get settled in a theater that oftentimes the group will miss the whole movie or everyone leaves without him.

Keywords for love are ***immature relationship style*** and, for money, ***projects*** and to ***study details.***

It has been my experience that if I see a reversed Page of Swords and it is a divorce situation, it can point out that there is at least one child very troubled by the situation who is acting out, possibly in destructive ways.

HOUSE NUMBER THREE, THE CUP FAMILY

This family is expert at caring for others. As mentioned earlier, the Wand family's yard is a bit of a mess, filled with dropped toys, bikes, and unfinished projects. Also remember the Sword family, sporting their neutral, shabby chic, and thoughtful yet uninspired yard. This deeply caring Cup family enjoys creating beautiful gathering places for everyone to enjoy. There will be a shade tree or pond feature with relaxing places to sit. There will be tables holding all sorts of comfort food made with love. The tree would be dressed and decorated in themes reflecting the current holiday. These welcoming people always seem to have cars outside their homes, filled with friends and family members stopping by to get a dose of loving support. They are involved in community action events and will add homemade food and loving charm to the block party. Inside there is a feeling of welcome, and the home will be comfortable and warm. The children are sensitive and may seem emotionally fragile. There will be plenty of food in the pantry, and extra umbrellas to hand to guests going out the door if it starts to rain while they're visiting. This family will create a huge amount of food for dinner, with the intention to share with neighbors who they feel need looking out for. Doing for others takes priority, and much of the time housekeeping is at a steady level of comfortable and tidy.

Think of any career where people are helping others, and I will show you a member of the Cup family. They're the first to help a neighbor with a project, and much of the time help doesn't even have to be requested. If they see you planting in your garden, someone from this family will bring a visor band for your eyes to keep the sun out, a bottle of water, and a compliment regarding your efforts. You'll have an opportunity to tell them all your gardening plans and how work is going for you and how your parents are and—well, you get the picture.

King of Cups
N

This is a man who expresses his wisdom through the filter of emotional warmth and sincere respect for the people struggling with life. He is creative and outgoing; however, because he is the patriarch of emotion, he's easily hurt and tends to remain sensitive toward a person or incident that caused him concern. In other words, he is able to put himself into another's shoes and work on tough situations such as relationships or community causes. This is a man who can listen well but also needs to be listened to. If he feels he hasn't been cared for by others, he has been known to pout and be a bit unreasonable and narcissistic when describing how horribly he feels he has been treated. He's the showman and is easily flattered. He is the one King in the deck who would find the single life unbearable.

Keywords regarding love describe him as a *kind* and *romantic man* and, for money, a *talented* and *helping man.*

Queen of Cups
N

She will be the first one to take your coat and get you a cup of tea when you drop by for a visit. She has an extra grace in her heart reserved just for the special treatment of children and animals. She is kind and generous and gives to others so often that she may betray her body and mind to the point of exhaustion. She has incredible intuition, fertility, and creativity that others envy and aspire to be like. She lives for family and community and will work tirelessly to see that an event is perfect for whoever is scheduled to be celebrated. She will remember birthdays and decorates for every holiday, creating a perfect meeting place for everyone.

Keywords for this beautiful Queen are *kind, romantic woman* and, for money, a very *talented* and *helping woman.*

Knight of Cups

This Knight represents a man or woman who is the archetypal romantic, with deep and strong emotions and a dramatic and creative personality. The leading man or woman in any movie where a charismatic personality is called for is the Knight of Cups. This card holds the most-passionate romantic energies, ones that can easily drift off into idealism and folly. Even with the risk of falling off the edge of the world in love, this Knight holds those magic moments, creating memories of promise to secure a lasting relationship. When these special loving moments are respectfully anchored and honored in a couple's declaration of truth, there will be no stopping them from success. All Knights are messengers, so with this particular Knight you will most likely receive messages of love in words or gifts from an admirer.

Keywords for love speak of a *loving message or person,* and for money, the keywords show *earning or spending on passions.*

Page of Cups
N

This card symbolizes a soft-spoken child who can be extremely sensitive and has poor boundaries. These children are very creative if they are lucky enough to be in a supportive family. Regarding self-expression, they will be directing plays and writing songs successfully before moving out of the house. In other words, these children have a certain level of success, due to their creativity, prior to leaving home. All Pages represent innocence and the beginning of something new. The Page of Cups can point to emotional immaturity specifically because of this person's deep sensitivities, which lead them into self-doubt and insecurity. If you draw this card while reading a mature developing relationship, it will give your client a peek into how their person of interest may react to harsh or direct tones. The world is a complicated and tough place to find peace for this susceptible one. This child or situation can be overly trusting and idealistic.

Keywords for love are simply ***timid love,*** and for money, keywords are ***new creative venture.***

HOUSE NUMBER FOUR, THE PENTACLE FAMILY

So, the yard of this home will be quite beautiful, since this family values nice things. The family can afford to hire professionals to landscape the yard; however, they have a deep respect for the earth and enjoy working the land, whether the space is large or small. Most often you will find a patch of yard devoted to growing food, and the family enjoys sharing the bounty with friends and neighbors. These are people of few words, but what they do say can be profound. They are slow to make decisions, appearing stubborn, and they never waste money and resources. As you may guess, change can be difficult with this family. Their professions are in banking, accounting, and securities of all kinds. They love the physical world, and healthcare would also be an enjoyable career path for them. Inside their home you'll find name-brand furnishings that are well cared for and dust-free. These will be pieces that are part of the family lineage, such as trust funds and a great-great-grand-aunt's quill pen, with inkwell preserved and proudly displayed. If there was a family business, there will be strong expectations, with the assumption of handing it down to the young ones like the generation before it. This family is honest and you can trust the members to keep you inside their belt of security, as long as you show the same steadfast respect to them. This is a family of means, and they can be generous but for the most part respect every person's path toward security and will not give unsolicited advice. The advice they do give is useful, and any money you may ask to borrow needs to be paid back on time; make no mistake, there will be added interest.

King of Pentacles

N

This is a man who is most often honest with conservative values and deep affection for the material aspect of life. This card represents security and stability and a man who respects nature. He doesn't find change, large or small, a comfortable process at all and will be stubborn with suggestions that pull him out of his comfort zone. He prides himself on his authority, and if perhaps his wisdom is not heeded or respected, he will quietly dismiss you and retreat into silence. When this card represents a situation, you can be sure it is asking you to use common sense regarding all practical matters. He's a person of wealth whom you can depend on, but is not as generous as, say, the King of Cups would be. If you borrow you will be expected to pay it back with interest.

Keywords for love are *status* and *secure love* and, for money, *secure position* and *status.*

Queen of Pentacles

N

This woman is a feminine reflection of the King, but with much more creativity and management skills. She may volunteer at community events and fundraisers or any projects that have the potential to bear tangible results. She is comfortable with the earth as well as her body. She is much like the Empress in the Major Arcana in regard to opportunities and generosity. She is a woman who is comfortable with all aspects of the material, so you will find her working in nature as a profession or helping others with their bodies in practical and traditional ways. Scientific facts and data can be her foundation of traditional medicine as well as natural remedies. She is a master of the unseen as long as results manifest in a timely manner.

Keywords for love are **sincere, practical,** and **realistic lover** and, for money, **partnerships** and **helping others.**

Knight of Pentacles

N

This is an active person who enjoys physical activities, preferably outside, where she or he can run on the earth. This card brings messages of new work or a new stream of income and can also point to travel for work or business. Money and status mean a lot to this person, which is how he brings the determination and tenacity to work hard and succeed, whether for himself as a sole owner in business or key point person in a corporation. It doesn't matter what is required to earn and enjoy desired possessions; this person will achieve these goals. In other words, unlike the traits in the other suits, this is the person who's most comfortable with delayed gratification and will patiently get the schooling and the certificates necessary to achieve what they want.

Keywords for love are ***stable and loyal partner*** and, for money, ***promotion*** and ***financial career.***

Page of Pentacles

N

This card represents a child who is curious about the world and is happy exploring and researching their particular interests for hours. Nature is very calming to these children. They love acquiring resources, whether intellectual facts about the world or physical items such as toys they really enjoy. If the question is about job and career and this card shows up, it means the beginning of a pathway to money or an internship of some kind. To be sure, this person is intelligent and ambitious. If I am answering a question about love, this Page may indicate meeting someone at work or someone who understands your industry. If this is representing a dependent child, then this is a young one who needs facts; things need to make sense to her/him. If you ask him to do something and he can't see the reasoning of why the task needs to be done, you can be sure he will keep digging for the answer. They will have a hard time doing something just for the sake of doing it.

Keywords for love are **meeting through work, practical, not romantic**, and, for money, **study finances, business, and healthcare.**

THE MAJOR ARCANA

PART THREE

There are 22 Major Arcana cards (*arcana* meaning "greater secrets" or "mysteries"). While the Minor Arcana, with the numbered cards (ace through 10) and the court cards represent the day-to-day life and the people in it, the Major Arcana speaks of the higher principles and morals a person aspires to. When major cards show up, it is spirit asking you to take a different perspective, a higher seat in the stadium, a progressive cord or tone in regard to your current situation. It's spirit saying, "Note well" and "Perhaps look at your situation from this angle." These are the messages that, once heeded, make each path in life a bit easier and help keep you off the ones suspended in a perpetual cycle of confusion. Major cards bring about higher thinking and give messages about your best purpose and life path at the moment. They shine a light and celebrate the best within you or point directly to blocks or restrictions that might be holding you back. The journey of this arcanum will start with a newborn (the Fool) and end with the wise one (the World). Each succeeding card represents one step closer to wholeness and alignment to who we are at soul level. Each card in this lineup represents a lesson that needs to be learned before moving to the next lesson in life, starting with the light-hearted Fool.

0. THE FOOL
Y

The Fool opens the journey as the true and full expression of a novice's heart. Even though this represents a childlike state of innocence, it is not meant to degrade or demean a person or situation. The Fool points to something fresh and new, absent of hardship, so there is zero bitterness, zero fear, and zero apprehensions. This is the energetic spirit holding the closest seat to God and angels. When the Fool enters a reading, it signals a joyous diversion from life, with many unexpected blessings and light-hearted shifts in thinking. The Fool card is a blessing representing miracles and welcomed surprises of good fortune. It's with a Fool's heart that the experience of true bliss is available.

Keywords for love are *new love or deepening of relationship* and, for money, *new job* and cautions to *spend wisely,* reminding you that you're the *novice.*

1. THE MAGICIAN
Y

The Magician plainly shows that you have all you need to proceed with any task or acquisition... except for maybe a bit of confidence. You may notice when looking at the image on this card that the elements of all suits (Wands, Swords, Cups, and Pentacles) are represented, and the Magician in you can handle them like an expert. This is the ultimate manifestation card encouraging you to tap into your spiritual gifts to bring in whatever you desire. This card says life is giving you special powers at this time. Draw on your intuition and mix it into your practical knowledge to manifest your dreams. Your thoughts create emotion that will create impulses to action, and the only way you can change your life is through action. Change doesn't live inside our wishes and hopes, which are only a part of the magic; it's *action* that brings in manifestation. Just like the image, you need to employ all aspects of your talents and abilities to be successful.

Keywords for love are **a strong spiritual connection** as well as **intuition** and, for money, **trust intuition** and you can **manifest quickly.**

2. THE HIGH PRIESTESS
Y

This beautiful being is the governess of your intuition. She knows everything but will share only what you need in each moment, and will guide you through the whispers of intuition. Seeing this card in your reading should encourage you to trust your gut, since this wise spirit is now close to you. Intuition does not speak through extreme emotion; it communicates through all your senses. Of course, emotions will play a part; however, if you don't have a physical impression through one or more of your chakras (the seven spiritual power points held in the body) and if you tune out listening to wise advice from your fellow humans, you will make choices that will ultimately confuse and untie the tangible supply you had hoped to secure. She is feminine power and the inner life of spirituality. It's been my experience that when the High Priestess comes into a reading regarding a relationship, it most often shows that the person you are reading for is looking for a deeper spiritual union than what they have had in the past.

Keywords for love are ***romantic yet not well grounded*** and, for money, ***take advantage of inner knowing.***

3. THE EMPRESS

Y

This card brings the existential down to Mother Earth, the divine feminine creator of all life. She masters creation on all levels, from procreation to the comforts of a happy home. While the High

Priestess creates spiritual power, our Empress is in charge of the material portion of our choices. You will most often see the Empress pictured sitting in nature, since that is her domain. Whether she appears in love or business, she is the ultimate feminine authority since she feeds all outside information through the filters of caring, nurturing, supporting others and brings in the best for all, not only the one. She asks you to have good questions in the moment, framed well. "What's your fascination and will you follow it?" "Are you nurtured enough to nurture others?" She reminds you that creativity will lift sadness and worry.

Keywords for this beautiful card regarding a love question are *mutual trust* and *affection* and can indicate *pregnancy*; for money, *good fortune, options,* and *success.*

4. THE EMPEROR

Y

The Emperor is the patriarch of mature masculine leadership in regard to the material world. Whereas the Empress is the creator of nature, the Emperor is the creator of industry, the military, and social leadership. When the Emperor appears, you should look at any issues or challenges you may be having concerning authority and understand that whoever this person may be in your life, please refrain from thinking of her/him as an oppressor or bully. This person really does want the best for you, even though your feelings are hurt or ego is bruised; they are wiser than you may give them credit for.

If appearing in your reading, this card means that following a level-headed and practical path will serve you well.

Keywords for love are ***stable, mature love with loyalty*** and, for money, ***success in business or legal matters***.

5. THE HIEROPHANT
Y

So, to review a moment, the Empress has dominion over the laws of nature and the Emperor is the keeper of traditional protocol regarding the financial industry and big corporations. Within the same line of thinking, this card, the Hierophant, holds leadership in our religious industries, representing the man-made churches with their various man-made interpretations of the Bible and other sacred texts.

When doing a love reading and a lady is interested in finding out more about someone she just met, and the Hierophant comes in to play, it's important to take note whether this card lands upright or reverse. Upright will mean that the person in question leans more toward traditional religious values held in society. In other words, a person who adheres to societal norms of timing in relationships will court a person for a certain amount of time, then become exclusive with that person, then engaged, and then married. If perhaps the

Hierophant hits the reading reversed, it has been my experience that the person in question is either not interested in a progressive relationship toward marriage, or quite simply the dating relationship has not matured enough for the card to appear upright. That means she or he may very well enjoy the thought of marriage in the future, but the situation at the moment hasn't grown strong enough in the energy signature to have it show up in the reading.

Keywords for love are **traditional thinking about relationships** and, for money, t**raditional ideas and culture** and **corporations**.

6. THE LOVERS
Y

The Lovers card shines the light on all collaboration that has a passionate component to it. Because of the title, most people see this as only meaning passionate sexual love, and indeed there is room for this interpretation; however, a broader perspective would serve you well since this card truly symbolizes a peace-filled collaboration between opposites and a clearing up of discrepancies within disputes. When reading a love question such as "I met this guy four weeks ago, and I want to know how he feels about our relationship," one card will not be enough to answer this to get the full picture of the situation. If I see the Lovers card, I can assume there is a healthy degree of sexual attraction for my client. However, if I don't see cards around the Lovers supporting emotional love (Cups), then it is my interpretation that his level of devotion is more superfluous and purely physical at this time. It could very well be that his feelings of deep emotional love have not yet eclipsed the raw physical attraction, and there may be an uneven sentimental investment on his part regarding this intimate union. To be clear, when reading this particular card and for many questions about love, you will need to look at supporting or contradicting cards to make sure you are intuiting the full picture for your client.

Keywords for love are *mutual caring and attraction* and, for money, *combine resources* and *collaborations.*

7. THE CHARIOT

Y

The Chariot can mean travel and transportation overland. It means fast-moving energy toward a goal, as long as both your horses are pointed in the same direction. As metaphor moves into literal, most decks depict this card with two different-colored animals representing opposing forces that you, as the driver, need to somehow join into a common ambition or objective to create success. This card appearing in the reading tells you that you can achieve success through shear willpower and control, which admittedly takes intense focus and discipline. This card shows you can master opposing forces in a fractured team at work or a broken family situation and bring them together. Like many of us, our own struggle with challenges is what enslaves us, not the situation itself.

Keywords for love are **self-care instead of chasing love** and, for money, **don't rush, just guide in steady ways.**

8. STRENGTH
Y

Strength gives you energy to endure and overcome deficiency and frailties. Kait has adorned this card with a beautiful woman who, through grace and patience, has tamed a lion. This card acknowledges the difficulties and suffering you have endured in discovering your inner strength and, to this end, an excellence in moral courage. You have tamed the beast within, not by force but by gentleness. Whenever this beautiful card shows in a reading, it indicates spirit asking you, as a reader, to tell the client that their efforts have been noticed by the higher powers and that they have earned an unspoiled thread of grace that will never leave.

Keywords for love are **you are aligning now, be patient** and, for money, **strong position or sound venture.**

9. THE HERMIT
Y

The Hermit is a soul in solitude; however, this solitude is not an option but spirit insisting you retreat into the silence of good council and spiritual contemplation. If you betray this request from the higher ups and instead power through with the business of your day, you will feel like you're faking it. You attend events or do your work with a feeling of being an imposter, a plastic shell. To rise above the empty feeling of this particular life rhythm, it would serve you well to withdraw from activities and distractions of the world. This is critical to understand who you are at soul level in relation to everything in your life. At times (looking at the other cards in the throw), the Hermit shows up in a reading and isn't asking the client to withdraw from all activity but rather offers a caution for her/him to hold back from chasing after a specific friend, concept, or project at this time.

If reading a person of interest for a client and the question is "We had a fight and I haven't heard from her/him for days—should I contact them?," the Hermit in the reading is saying no. To follow this person into their private spiritual solitude will never prove fruitful. Look for your own council of teachers and guides. It's smart of you to turn off music and shutter outside noises as best as you can, to hear the soft whispers of advice and guidance.

Keywords for love are **needing time alone** and **more independence.** For money, **seek counsel from wise ones.**

10. THE WHEEL OF FORTUNE

Y

The Wheel represents the cycles of life and shows that an uptick in good fortune is coming your way. It's the ultimate good-luck card and always a pleasant and welcome sight in a reading. You have put something in motion (you may or may not remember what it is) that will be paying off. This says destiny has orchestrated (most often) an unexpected and positive turn of events. If reversed or if the supporting cards are negative, it doesn't necessarily mean the good fortune isn't available, but more that the client is doing something to sabotage the situation and dodging this influential destiny. Are you so comfortable with the known that you are turning away from something new? Or is it your low self-esteem making you feel like an unworthy benefactor of such good fortune? Something to think about.

Keywords for love are *enjoy an improvement in relationships* and, for money, *what's in motion brings success.*

11. JUSTICE
Y

Justice speaks to you about the legal matters in your life, from the simple handshake agreements to binding contracts and all matters of the court, be they civil or criminal. It asks you to look at all the facts and weigh them *fairly* against one another to reach balanced conclusions. This card suggests you are calm and deliberate when taking any action. It is a reminder to allow enough time to ensure that fair-minded decisions are offered or executed. Divide equally all property, money, or settlements. If perhaps Justice is reversed, it has been my experience that the person you're reading for may feel they are on the unfair or unjust side of a decision or situation. They may feel angry or resentful, and the supporting cards in the reading will tell you the full story. If Justice is reversed, it commonly means a delay in the process. If paired with Pentacles, most often it represents documents, and the specific Pentacle will tell you what kind. For instance, if the 10 of Pentacles stands with Justice, then most often it is contracts with family or inheritance. If paired with the Hierophant or Empress, most often I read this as a marriage document or birth certificate.

Keywords for love are ***seeking balance and fairness*** and, for money, ***fair financial settlement is reached.***

12.
THE HANGED MAN
Y

The Hanged Man is also known as the Hanging Man, picturing a person upside down who is feeling stuck and can't make a decision. This represents someone trying their best to see the problem from a different direction so they can have all the information before moving forward. This card is much like the Hermit because of its solitary nature; however, the difference is that the Hermit is life *insisting* you stop and separate yourself from everything to gain spiritual knowledge, and the Hanged Man says *you are choosing* to stop and separate from all to achieve a different perspective regarding situations, people, and projects. The Hanged Man means surrendering your desired control over outcomes, most often indicating the letting go of old patterns that aren't serving you now. In the past these gave you a sense of security, but now, to stay true to yourself, you choose differently. If perhaps this card lands in reverse, it indicates that clients are most likely resisting the necessary changes to move forward and end up just leaving themselves and others hanging in the wind. Of all the readings I have done on love, the reversed Hanged Man most often represents a partner acting immaturely both socially and emotionally in regard to the situation at hand. If for money, it can show good old-fashioned stubbornness on the client's part. This makes YOU, the reader, the person life has picked to point out new ways of thinking to ultimately encourage her/him to make choices that will better serve them.

Keywords for love are ***you or your partner releases control and ego*** and, for money, ***changing mind about money, career, or job.***

13. DEATH
Y

The Death card means the ending of a cycle, not literally the ending of life. This card tells you to release the past, take time to mourn it, and then move forward to a fresh new beginning. This is a time where change can't be avoided; when it is upon you and you're going through the letting-go process, this card promises that something better is coming soon. Spirit never allows bad to happen where good can't come of it. Look at all aspects of life, job, and career as well as friends and family and study the ones that make your edges feel tired and worn out. Look also at how you behave or interact with these souls. Is it time to let go of what you think you know, and embrace a new way of living? Your old ways and treatment of others may need to die for the blessing of a lighter version of you to finally reveal itself and serve the world as intended in your soul's blueprint.

Keywords for love are ***changing old patterns of behavior*** and, for money, ***changing the way you handle money.***

14. TEMPERANCE
Y

Temperance means moderation and advises you not to get off your horse, and to ride in the middle lane for the day. Be measured in your actions and keep your nose out of everybody else's business. Don't push your opinion on anyone and don't move close to the edges for debate on any topic; in other words, *temper your ego.* She represents the constant interaction of the spiritual and material worlds, an ongoing process to raise the dense earth while mixing the blessings of heaven, creating the promised equilibrium between good and evil so that we—inside our human experience—can enjoy the power of choice. When this card appears, she is advising you to watch and learn from others without filters or bias, since there is something valuable for you in whatever is going on for you right now. At this moment in time, you are the student, not the teacher.

Keywords for love are **heal rifts and avoid ego now** and, regarding money, **cooperation and peace in the workplace.**

15. THE DEVIL
Y

This is a card that affects all other cards around it in a negative way, pouring a dark shadow on everything because it signals addiction of all kinds. It's about feeling enslaved and fixated by your choice of (the short list includes) drugs, alcohol, overeating, shopping, or depending on anger and violence to dominate how you get your way with others. The Devil shows you when you may be obsessing over another person, project, or material thing. This card shows, in no uncertain terms, that your client or the person of interest is on a destructive path that will slow down all momentum for success and happiness. It is part of the social and ethical equilibrium that Temperance speaks of, and when you see this in a throw, it says to pay attention to your thoughts because not all of them will be your own. Be on notice that something may be carrying you away, and it's time to self-reflect and course-correct. As with any addiction that can overwhelm and hijack the emotional integrity of a family, workplace, and personal life, it is clear you may not be in as much control as you thought. If I'm doing a love reading and the client is asking about a loved one, I tread lightly because the client sometimes won't recognize the problem if they have been living with it for a while. We can become desensitized to the problem.

Keywords for love are ***obsessive, possibly harmful situation*** and, for money, ***attached to social and material status.***

16. THE TOWER
Y

The Tower is one of the most unwelcome cards since it represents unwelcomed change. Most books describe it as catastrophic ruin, since it points to sudden and swift changes that go against our human nature of striving to live within a sense of security at all costs. As ominous as this sounds, I have discovered that most readings containing the Tower show that my client has an intense desire to control a situation that *isn't supposed to be manifested*, and a change in perspective now can offset harsher life lessons down the way. The Tower can indeed signal a sudden job loss or accident that causes financial stress and will set on fire any and all worn-out structures that aren't serving you any longer. This card demands that you pay attention and free yourself from the prison you have put yourself in. You need to step back far enough to see if that job (the one you just got fired from) truly reflected your life's joy-filled fascinations. Most often I have found that long before you find yourself inside the turmoil of a Tower, it has whispered messages to course-correct, messages to reevaluate what you think you need in life to be happy. A visual I like to share regarding the Tower is one of God picking you up by the back of your collar and lifting you out of a comfortable situation (comfortable but not aligned to your soul's contract) and gently swinging you back and forth. Even though the movement feels unwanted at the time, you notice that all the devils that were insisting on strict rules of preservation start to fall away. As this situation calms, you start trusting that life is placing you where you are supposed to be, remembering that spirit never allows bad to happen that good won't come of it. Once your Tower has fallen, you can rebuild using only the bricks that will truly serve you this time. The bricks of faith, trust, and the ones you find by getting back to basics will most often lessen the impact. You can, with the information you receive in the reading (reflected in the surrounding cards), voluntarily dismantle your Tower (being open to new perspectives) and throw away the bricks that are threatening to fall anyway. One way or another, the bad bricks holding your Tower up will come down, either by your own choices or through the power you have bestowed your teachers, guardians, and guides from the beginning. Your agreement to live within your soul's blueprint matters most. You came to earth for a reason, and the Tower ensures you stay within the agreement set up for this lifetime.

Keywords regarding love are *stop old habits and ways regarding love* and, for money, *change attachment to wealth and status*.

17. THE STAR
Y

After the progression from addiction (Devil) to collapse (Tower), the Star comes in and gives hope after all the storms, and promises better days ahead. Your creativity comes back, along with new spiritual understanding, shifting life so the magic of synchronicities returns. The warm wind of hope is at your back, moving you gently forward. This card symbolizes an end to problems, the proverbial light at the end of the tunnel. You remember that your life's purpose manifests through the divine gifts you bring to the world, and now they begin to reveal themselves. The lessons learned from past trauma serve you well, and life will ensure that you will have opportunity to offer this wisdom to others. Every word is profound when the light of the Star is upon you.

Keywords for love are **hope for the future** and, for money, **improved wealth and recognition.**

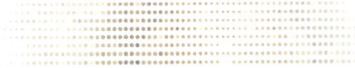

18. THE MOON
Y

The Moon is all about emotions and, with that, illusions. When this mysterious card appears, it's asking you to be mindful of your imagination, since you are now susceptible and vulnerable to fear-based thinking. You become more aware of your emotions, and your keen psychic abilities will reveal more options for your life. But be careful with those options and make sure that you are centered and clear before making your mind up. Moon is saying to sleep and center before deciding, since your emotions may be skewing the real picture, and your choice may not be viable in the light of day. This isn't a bad thing, because for writers and artists this is a time of increased imagination, so exploit it now for great success. Having the Moon card in your reading asks you to be quiet and watch people and dreams, understanding that decisions should be set aside for now since you just can't see the whole picture yet. Use this time instead to study the thread of light connecting you to others and to the heavenly resources.

Keywords for love are ***high emotions with some illusions*** and, for money, ***listen to intuition with work and projects.***

19. THE SUN
Y

The Sun comes next and fills those shadowy illusions the Moon was casting with light that reveals the truth of all things. This one will brighten up all other cards in the reading, lightening up the negative ones and giving added blessing to all others. The Sun splashes happiness, clarity, and a large dose of impulse for carefree self-expression. You have just breathed in the creative blessings of the Moon that the Sun will help you express in the written word, a dance, a canvas, a song, or a sweet cake. The world is anxious to see what you come up with, and you can trust your work will be received well. This is a great time to start new projects and get across the finish line. This is a time to prosper, so look toward the horizon and follow the light of the Sun.

Keywords for love are **happy relationship with bright future** and, for money, **period of prosperity, honors, and recognition.**

20. JUDGMENT
Y

This is known as the karma card, one of rejuvenation and healing. It has been my experience when reading about lost love that if the Judgment card shares time in your reading, the answer will be one of reunion and redemption. Judgment says you reap what you've sown, and all good actions spent in your relationship have accrued; the outcome will be in your favor. It is a time of healing and an awakening of self-realization; a rebirth. And with that, make the necessary adjustment to express who you truly are. The name of this card may give the impression that you are being judged, but it points more toward benefiting from your past work. No one outside of yourself is judging you. The Judgment card helps you back up far enough from any situation to see the perfection in it. It is the moment you realize that you are fine with or without a partner, since you know there are many souls attending you and steering you toward your divine path. Judgment asks you to look at your choices and life situation to determine what you will keep and what you don't want to live with anymore.

Keywords for love are **bring less judgment of self and others** and, for money, **choose a path that aligns with your talents.**

21. THE WORLD
Y

The World completes the road from the young novice with the Fool's heart to a well-rounded and wise conclusion described by the World. Completing the circle, you have picked up many things along your journey: lots of wisdom and mastery ending in great fortune. You have faced the dark side and danced on the razor's edge through each of the major cards, and this last card congratulates you for a job well done. You can rest with balance and wholeness from this expedition from innocence to enlightenment. If you see this card in your reading, it means you are aligned to your soul's destiny. Upright gives reassurance that whatever you focus on will prosper. If reversed or ill dignified, it will show that something is blocking the blessings being sent your way, whether you are conscious of it or not. The other cards in the reading will tell you what your blocks might be.

Keywords for love are a ***mature and fulfilling relationship*** and, for money, ***successfully reaching goals/travel.***

Properly framing the question is such an important part of a good reading. You never want to do a reading with an open-ended question. Make sure you are framing the question properly for yourself and your clients by adding a finite ending. Here are some good examples.

Instead of a client asking, "Will I ever marry?," reframe the question for your client with "Will I meet my love this summer?" Make sure you never set yourself up to answer a yes or no question with an absolute. You want to stay away from the words *never* and *always* in a reading. I feel it's arrogant, even disrespectful and could inadvertently take hope for the future away from the client. As good a reader as you may become, don't forget the element of free choice on the human side and miracles on the heavenly side that can change the future.

Questions from a client such as "Will I ever get rich?" should be reframed to something like "Will I hit my quarterly goals? If not, what can I do to better my chances for success?"

Asking, "Will my boyfriend ever come back?" should be changed to "How is he feeling about our relationship?"

A person shouldn't ask, "Will I ever be able to buy a house?" Better to ask, "When would be a good time for me to buy a house?"

Don't ask, "When am I going to die?" Better to ask, "How can I start living my best life?"

Another question clients ask is if they should stay in a challenging situation or leave. Get in the habit of telling them you don't tell people whom to leave and whom to stay with. A good advisor won't tell a person what to do. Answering this question for the client allows them to abdicate responsibility for their own life. Being clear and smart with the questions will ensure your answers are helpful, objective, and, most of all, empowering. Tell your client you won't make their mind up for them but will be able to tell them what the most probable future looks like if things don't change. Understanding what to expect next will give them the information needed to make their own decisions. Those seeking psychic guidance need an unbiased advisor to rely on.

FOLLOWING YOUR INTUITION IN READINGS

Be a balanced and grounded advisor by recognizing the differences between intuition and imagination. The *Clarity Tarot* can help you tune in to information through color and suit elements, keywords, and yes/no pointers, helping you continue working within your intuition and out of your imagination. Everyone's imagination is packed full of opinions, preferences, and thoughts that may lead an advisor to think thoughts such as "Well, if it were me in your situation, I would do it THIS way." This is never helpful to your client, since they don't call us to have us tell them what to do. They reached out for a message from spirit, not chitchat with friends. Clients come to you because they know that their friends have opinions and a vested interest that they stay within their own personal standards and expectations.

Tap into your intuition by developing a still-point practice. After throwing cards in a spread, silence your mind by focusing on commonalities, noticing what pairs up, such as a lot of the same numbers or a dominant color or suit. That alone can open your intuition and activate messages from spirit.

Are there more Wands (red/orange; fire element)? Then action is the still point and the door into your intuition. More Wands than any other suit means there are lots of moving parts or a flurry of action inside this situation. The specific card will tell you if your client is the one who should take action or if the situation is moving by itself.

More Pentacles (green; earth element)? Then acquisition and manifestation are the key to trigger your intuition. When Pentacles overwhelm the throw, there is surely some slow-moving energy, since this suit has the longest manifestation time. This full-bodied suit tells you that you will be rewarded through your tenacity.

More Swords (cool blue; air element; the mind)? Ah, go into your head and notice your thoughts is what spirit wants you to do. If there are more

Swords, you can be sure there's some over-thinking or analyzing. Learning how to properly frame a question will open a door to your intuition and take hold of the situation.

And finally, are the Cups (gold color; emotions) dominating the reading? Then in the beginning you will need to come from a heart connection. A reading with more Cups will indicate that a person may be making decisions based solely on a deep feeling, or the situation is so backed with emotions that it's moving into chaos. It's always in someone's best interest to make decisions with clear facts and not emotion.

Are there more low-numbered cards? Then you know that this problem or situation is new or has taken a new turn. Higher-numbered cards will lead your intuition to the assumption that this is an older pattern for the client or that the situation has been long standing.

To give a great reading, enter the stillness and hear, see, and feel the story. Here are a few other tips to keep in mind before you speak:

- Make sure the story makes sense and isn't fragmented or fractured with information that doesn't relate.

- If you are a visual person, ask yourself what pictures in your mind serve the conversation and which don't.

- Resist the abstract thought or image in your mind as relevant to the story. Stay in line with the conversation. If perhaps a random thought or image comes in, write it down to address later. Don't break up the smooth correspondence of taking one topic at a time with ideas that don't flow.

SPREADS AND THROWS

Spreads are the different ways we lay down cards, and they are also known as throws. There are many ways to cast a throw, and you can make up your own as well. The premise is that every card has a meaning or way it influences the topic or question by the position it is in. A common one, for example, is the past, present, and future three-card spread. The first card is the recent past (two to four weeks ago), the present card will tell the influences for the situation as it stands now, as well as what your impulses may be, and the third card shows what the next two to four weeks will bring. And of course, with that information you can decide a different plan of action if that most likely future isn't satisfying.

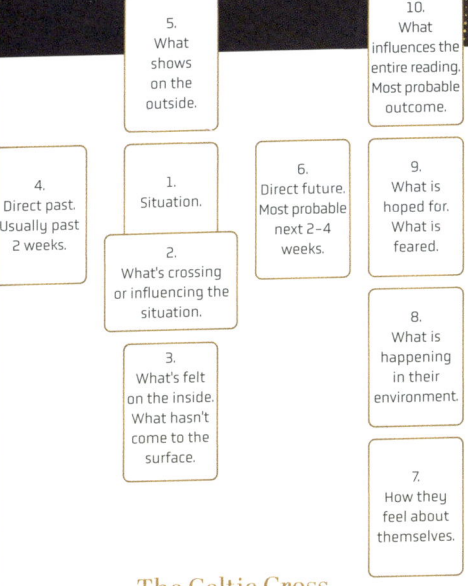

The Celtic Cross

This is my favorite spread since it will tell you the situation in a language that will be clearer than how the client is seeing it. Here is a template of my version of the Celtic Cross that I have found works best for me in my fast-paced practice.

Sometimes in challenging times with lots of confusion, clients can't find the words to describe their situation, and this throw will help clear everything up with the first card. In such cases, the Celtic Cross is the spread for you, since it tells you who or what the situation or person is influencing the situation. It also shows what the energies that brought the current events around (past two to four weeks). The Celtic Cross tells what the most probable future will be (next two to four weeks) and what the most probable future will be if no different action is taken. The seventh position reveals how clients are feeling about themselves. The next position shows how their environment is either supporting or not supporting them at this time. The environment position includes workplace as well as home. There is the hopes-and-fears position, which clearly shows if your client is feeling negatively or positively about the situation, and the last card gives you an overview of the entire reading.

Five-Card Yes/No

As mentioned in the Introduction, properly framing a yes or no question is the key to a successful reading. Draw five cards and add up how many cards have a Y at the top and how many have an N. You will have the answer. So, the professional way of doing this reading is if you know the answer the client is seeking is yes and the cards show a no, it's important that you don't just say, "No," and let hope fall from their heart. Here is an example of how to deliver not-so-good news:

Client: "My boyfriend and I had a fight. Will he contact me by the weekend?" The combination of cards laid down in front of you will tell you yes/no and why.

Here is an example of how to interpret this five-card lineup with the question "My boyfriend and I had a fight. Will he contact me by the weekend?"

- NO—5 of Cups
  (guilt and remorse regarding the situation)
- NO—9 of Swords
  (can't find the words and anxiety)
- YES—2 of Swords
  (stalemate, not moving forward)
- NO—7 of Cups
  (not all ideas are based in reality)
- NO—5 of Pentacles
  (worried about money/job)

As you can see, there are four no cards and one yes card, making the answer to her question no; however, it looks like there's a good reason. Her boyfriend is feeling bad about the fight, even to the point of losing sleep over it, but the most important reason is he can't find the words to start the conversation. Now that the client knows why she may not hear from him, she can now chose whether or not she wants to reach out first.

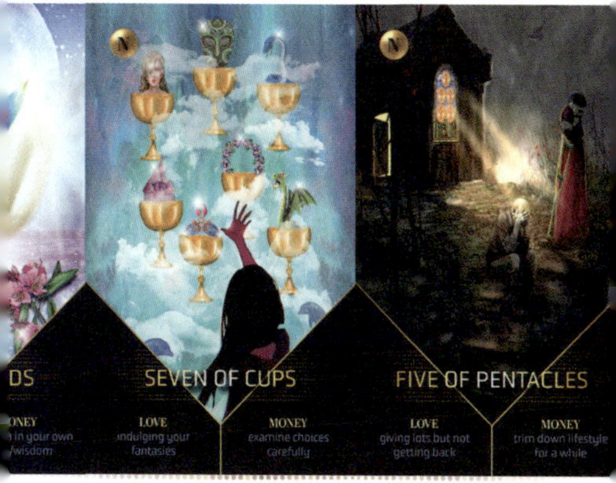

SEVEN OF CUPS		FIVE OF PENTACLES	
LOVE	MONEY	LOVE	MONEY
indulging your fantasies	examine choices carefully	giving lots but not getting back	trim down lifestyle for a while

Timing Spread

The timing spread is more a technique than a spread, and since it is one of the unique components of this deck, I want to tell you how to use it best. So, there are many ways to tell time with the Tarot, but this one has served me well. You shuffle the deck, laying down cards one at a time until you reach a major card. The number on the right side of that card will give you the timing. It is up to you to decide if the number represents days, weeks, or months. Some advisors may even want to predict hours. I enjoy the one-month increment, mentioning to the client that psychic timing can be tricky, so the client will need to know that it might take a couple of weeks. If perhaps the client feels it is too far away, look at the cards prior to the major one, since they may reveal some roadblocks. If the roadblock is the client getting in their own way, then you can suggest some changes to shorten or quicken the process to reach the goal faster.

CHEAT SHEET

Below, for quick reference, you will find a list of the keywords for each card.

ACE OF WANDS—N—Love: *new joy/love/creativity.* **Money:** *profits/creative projects.*

2 OF WANDS—Y—Love: *building a rewarding relationship.* **Money:** *beneficial guidance from others.*

3 OF WANDS—N—Love: *commitment/engagement/celebration.* **Money:** *efforts bear fruit/others help.*

4 OF WANDS—Y—Love: *happy/comfortable home/contentment.* **Money:** *success/harmony/stability.*

5 OF WANDS—N—Love: *bickering/let go of ego.* **Money:** *tensions at work/gossip.*

6 OF WANDS—Y—Love: *time of happiness/encouragement.* **Money:** *well-deserved success/you are being noticed.*

7 OF WANDS—N—Love: *big ego/try seeing the other's side.* **Money:** *hold your ground/diligent work.*

8 OF WANDS—Y—Love: *sudden interest/fast and passionate.* **Money:** *split-second decisions/rapid gains.*

9 OF WANDS—N—Love: *resolving challenges with partner.* **Money:** *the worst is over/stability ahead.*

10 OF WANDS—Y—Love: *support partner in hard time/uneven care.* **Money:** *have taken on too much/feelings of burnout.*

KING OF WANDS—N—Love: *affectionate and passionate man.* **Money:** *good fortune through action.*

QUEEN OF WANDS—N—Love: *romantic/loyal/always busy.* **Money:** *creative woman/do what you love.*

KNIGHT OF WANDS—N—Love: *enjoyable/uncommitted affair.* **Money:** *take the risk/action is favored.*

PAGE OF WANDS—N—Love: *playful/honest relationship.* **Money:** *new skill or investment.*

ACE OF SWORDS—N—Love: *rising above adversity/healing.* **Money:** *inspiration/possible new job/clarity.*

2 OF SWORDS—Y—Love: *time for balanced thinking on situation.* **Money:** *have faith in your own ideas/wisdom.*

3 OF SWORDS—N—**Love:** *quarreling, but union worth saving.* **Money:** *loss of trust/unhappy job.*

4 OF SWORDS—Y—**Love:** *much-needed time for self.* **Money:** *rest after hard work/burnout.*

5 OF SWORDS—N—**Love:** *arguing is not the answer/careful.* **Money:** *avoid arguments and enemies.*

6 OF SWORDS—Y—**Love:** *moving into calmer waters/cooperation.* **Money:** *work situation improving.*

7 OF SWORDS—N—**Love:** *seek compromise/use diplomacy.* **Money:** *warns about moving forward/risk is high.*

8 OF SWORDS—Y—**Love:** *feeling you have no choice/trapped.* **Money:** *fear of change/hands are tied.*

9 OF SWORDS—N—**Love:** *feeling rejected/lonely/undervalued.* **Money:** *regret and anxiety/feeling drained.*

10 OF SWORDS—Y—**Love:** *strain from caring for others.* **Money:** *feel under pressure and suspicious.*

KING OF SWORDS—N—**Love:** *intellectual man/not romantic.* **Money:** *take-charge leader/is direct.*

QUEEN OF SWORDS—N—Love: *smart/independent woman.* **Money:** *educated powerhouse.*

KNIGHT OF SWORDS—N—Love: *shifts in relationship.* **Money:** *finance/job shift.*

PAGE OF SWORDS—N—Love: *immature relationship style.* **Money:** *projects/study details.*

ACE OF CUPS—N—Love: *a new path to love/passion/purpose.* **Money:** *new creative job/project fulfillment.*

2 OF CUPS—Y—Love: *harmony/balance/mutual respect.* **Money:** *financial partnerships/you inspire.*

3 OF CUPS—N—Love: *socializing with friends/kindred spirits.* **Money:** *profits through group efforts.*

4 OF CUPS—Y—Love: *withdrawing affections/indifference.* **Money:** *attached to money and security.*

5 OF CUPS—N—Love: *regret/remorse/resentment.* **Money:** *unfulfilled/don't throw good money after bad.*

6 OF CUPS—Y—Love: *reunions/life improves/old friends and family.* **Money:** *renewed enthusiasm/improved finances.*

7 OF CUPS—N—Love: *indulging your fantasies.* **Money:** *examine choices carefully.*

8 OF CUPS—Y—Love: *walking away from love/ project.* **Money:** *cut your losses and conserve.*

9 OF CUPS—N—Love: *rewarding love/ contentment.* **Money:** *new job/position or promotion.*

10 OF CUPS—Y—Love: *a loving/joyful relationship.* **Money:** *rewards/respect/success.*

KING OF CUPS—N—Love: *kind/romantic man.* **Money:** *talented/helping man.*

QUEEN OF CUPS—N—Love: *kind/romantic woman.* **Money:** *talented/helping woman.*

KNIGHT OF CUPS—N—Love: *loving messages.* **Money:** *a passionate venture.*

PAGE OF CUPS—N—Love: *timid love.* **Money:** *earning or spending on passions.*

ACE OF PENTACLES—N—Love: *meet through work/practical person.* **Money:** *practical venture/profits.*

2 OF PENTACLES—Y—Love: *shared resources/ working with love partner.* **Money:** *juggling projects in collaboration.*

3 OF PENTACLES—N—Love: *stay positive work through your differences.* **Money:** *good at your work/people notice.*

4 OF PENTACLES—Y—Love: *stable/secure/ love and status.* **Money:** *play it safe/secure job.*

5 OF PENTACLES—N—Love: giving lots but not getting back. **Money:** trim down lifestyle for a while.

6 OF PENTACLES—Y—Love: sharing resources/both benefit. **Money:** financial backing/teamwork.

7 OF PENTACLES—N—Love: small steps to improvement. **Money:** starting to see gains/ don't give up.

8 OF PENTACLES—Y—Love: dedicated to each other/mature love. **Money:** getting a raise/ respect/gains.

9 OF PENTACLES—N—Love: content with or without a partner. **Money:** acquire property/ profit/retirement.

10 OF PENTACLES—Y—Love: secure family life legacy. **Money:** wealth, family/inheritance.

KING OF PENTACLES—N—Love: status/secure love. **Money:** secure position/status.

QUEEN OF PENTACLES—N—Love: sincere/ practical/realistic lover. **Money:** partnerships/ helping others.

KNIGHT OF PENTACLES—N—Love: stable/ loyal partner. **Money:** promotion/financial career.

PAGE OF PENTACLES—N—Love: meeting through work/practical/not romantic. **Money:** study finances/business/healthcare.

0. FOOL—Y—**Love:** *new love or deepening of relationship.* **Money:** *new job/spend wisely/novice.*

1. MAGICIAN—Y—**Love:** *a strong spiritual connection/intuition.* **Money:** *trust intuition/can manifest quickly.*

2. HIGH PRIESTESS—Y—**Love:** *romantic yet not well grounded.* **Money:** *take advantage of inner knowing.*

3. EMPRESS—Y—**Love:** *mutual trust/affection/pregnancy.* **Money:** *good fortune/options/success.*

4. EMPEROR—Y—**Love:** *stable/mature love with loyalty.* **Money:** *success in business or legal matters.*

5. HIEROPHANT—Y—**Love:** *traditional thinking about relationships.* **Money:** *traditional ideas and culture/corporations.*

6. LOVERS—Y—**Love:** *mutual caring and attraction.* **Money:** *combine resources/collaborations.*

7. CHARIOT—Y—**Love:** *self-care instead of chasing love.* **Money:** *don't rush/just guide in steady ways.*

8. STRENGTH—Y—**Love:** *you are aligning now/ be patient.* **Money:** *strong position or sound venture.*

9. HERMIT—Y—Love: *needing time alone/more independence.* **Money:** *seek counsel from wise ones.*

10. WHEEL OF FORTUNE—Y—Love: *enjoy an improvement in relationships.* **Money:** *what's in motion brings success.*

11. JUSTICE—Y—Love: *seeking balance and fairness.* **Money:** *fair financial settlement is reached.*

12. HANGED MAN—Y—Love: *you or your partner release control and ego.* **Money:** *changing mind about money, career/job.*

13. DEATH—Y—Love: *changing old patterns of behaviors.* **Money:** *changing the way you handle money.*

14. TEMPERANCE—Y—Love: *heal rifts and avoid ego now.* **Money:** *cooperation and peace in workplace.*

15. DEVIL—Y—Love: *obsessive/possibly harmful situation.* **Money:** *attached to social and material status.*

16. TOWER—Y—Love: *stop old habits and ways regarding love.* **Money:** *change attachment to wealth and status.*

17. STAR—Y—Love: *hope for the future.* **Money:** *improved wealth and recognition.*

18. MOON—Y—Love: *high emotions with some illusions.* **Money:** *listen to intuition with work and projects.*

19. SUN—Y—Love: *happy relationship with bright future.* **Money:** *period of prosperity/honors/recognition.*

20. JUDGMENT—Y—Love: *bring less judgment of self and others.* **Money:** *choose a path that aligns with your talents.*

21. WORLD—Y—Love: *a mature and fulfilling relationship.* **Money:** *successfully reaching goals/travel.*

SERVING THE WORLD

There are so many different ways that you can give others great insight, I thought that you would enjoy learning the ways you can work as a professional. To that end, I'm listing many of the different jobs I perform. You may see yourself serving the world with a career as a Tarot specialist.

Hotline Advisor

Loving the Tarot guided me to explore life as an online advisor. They aren't like they used to be, with shady personal chats. New regulations and serious advisors have insisted that the platforms are of high principles. For the most part, the ones with high integrity will have a wonderful customer service department that is attentive both to clients and advising staff.

I give fast answers ensuring the most value to my clients, but sometimes when reading late in the evening I would catch myself drifting off into imagination instead of intuition. I love working, even when I feel a bit tired, so to stay centered and in good company, I developed this deck. This is to support not only myself to stay within my own standards of integrity, but my fellow hotline advisors as well as my students. Now you can enjoy staying on track, using the many unique components added to this deck. Serving with sincerity is paramount to me, and I know it is for you as well.

I have achieved high status with proven accuracy on top sites and enjoy giving quick and concise readings to my clients. In fact, the reason I created this deck is for the person like me who wants to do a lot of readings back to back and may struggle staying centered when working long hours. It can feel like I've lost the connection to spirit. The images and text in this deck will keep a reader on the right track no matter how long they've been reading the Tarot.

Event Psychic

Even though I take the psychic sciences seriously, there is nothing more fun than working at an event. Large and small businesses as well as corporations will hire me to join their celebration. I'm part of the entertainment, giving readings for up to six hours in one event. This is something the host will pay for, and all readings are free for the guests. This is a fast-paced party where I do readings one on one in a semiprivate setting.

At times I'm asked to dress in a theme to match the event, but I draw the line at turbans, crystal balls, and black cats! My table is sometimes placed between the balloon animal man and the face painter, but I don't mind. These events are always fun, but I keep in mind that no matter how lighthearted I present myself, a reading is always serious business to the person sitting across from me.

My guest client will always remember what I say to them, and the line for my readings goes out the door and around the room. People have missed their entire party just waiting in line for their turn. During an event like this, using the *Clarity Tarot*, it's important that my readings are full bodied and presented in two to three minutes, enabling about 25 guests an hour to have a reading. Because I am face to face with the person, I can show them the images on the cards, and they are able to understand all the information no matter how fast it's coming.

Stage Entertainer

Stage work is when there are small- to medium-sized salons for groups of people who would like a mix of what I do and how I do it. Some are privately hosted and some are events I put on myself, where a limited number of tickets are available. I offer messages from passed loved ones as well as spirit guide readings. Usually more than one person in the group will be benefiting from a message. I use some of the time explaining how the average person can see spirit, develop their intuition, and understand signs from the other side. I try to keep the size of each group small enough so everyone will get a message.

Animal Communication

It's easier than you may think to understand your beloved pets by using our deck. Your frame of reference needs to have a different starting point, since you are reading a living spirit that doesn't have the capacity to make its own choices other than the ones that are naturally in its nature. When an animal lives its life close to humans, it can pick up curious idiosyncrasies that may feel very complex. To get to the bottom of problematic behaviors, we need to understand that this beautiful little being has a kind and loving heart, and an innocence that we sometimes take for granted.

FINAL WORDS

I realize that learning something new takes discipline and effort, and to keep things moving forward I have videos online to help you. I'm passionate about teaching others how to serve people who are challenged by a situation and need competent counsel to get them out of the pain and relieve the stress of uncertainty. Sharing a person's most probable future trajectory takes away some surprises and lowers anxiety or encourages certain action to be able to change course, to ease through a challenge with less suffering. Either way, you are empowering another with good information from the good company of the higher frequencies. With sincerity of purpose, I hope you find as much satisfaction in your life as I have in mine, helping others.

Kait and I have enjoyed creating this deck for you. The keywords give you a jump start toward developing your own truth and a personal journey of helping others with the Tarot.

There are many ways to read the Tarot, and I encourage you to stick with one system until you understand it, mind, body, and spirit. Listening to many different theories can be frustrating. As time goes on, you will start to hear your own voice. And with that, I want you to know I'm here to help.

With deep respect for your path.
DEBRA ZACHAU